ARUNACHALA : "THE HILL OF THE HOLY BEACON"

A MESSAGE FROM ARUNACHALA

A MESSAGE FROM ARUNACHALA

By

Paul Brunton

PILGRIMS

PILGRIMS PUBLISHING

◆ Varanasi ◆

A MESSAGE FROM ARUNACHALA

By
Paul Brunton

Published by:
PILGRIMS PUBLISHING

An imprint of:
PILGRIMS BOOK HOUSE
(Distributors in India)
B 27/98 A-8, Nawabganj Road
Durga Kund, Varanasi-221010, India
Tel: 91-542-2314060
Fax: 2312456
E-mail: pilgrims@satyam.net.in
Website: www.pilgrimsbooks.com

Cover Design by Roohi Burchett

ISBN: 978-81-7769-785-8

Printed in India at Pilgrim Press Pvt. Ltd. Lalpur Varanasi

About the Author

Paul Brunton was born in 1898 in Britain. He soon forsook a career in journalism to travel east, where he sought the company of yogis, mystics, holy men and philosophers. As he bathed in the glow and spiritual atmosphere, he was consumed by the ideas of these people. So strong were his impressions and experiences in the company of these learned and wise men, that he spent the rest of his life writing about the gifts that had been taught him.

He was one of the first writers to explore the wisdom of the eastern mystics. In the various books he wrote, he made an attempt to enlighten others about the powers of the mind. He realised that one must shun the external world and look more deeply into one's own mind. Do his profuse writings provide true answers to those vexing questions of man: who am I, and what is my true consciousness?

Paul Brunton had a great talent for making his points concise and readable. He elucidates his theme clearly, for this topic is not one that is easily conveyed. Using a western perspective, in all his books he opens a window on the apparently mysterious ideas of the mystics and yogis of the east. He died in 1981.

FOREWORD

BY
SIR VEPA RAMESAN, KT., B.A., B.L.
Retired Acting Chief Justice, High Court of Madras

The name Paul Brunton needs no introduction to English readers; wherever the English language is read—in England, in America and in India alike—his books have been widely read, and have made men pause and think that possibly mankind is on the verge of getting a new knowledge.

The present book is a natural sequel to those three works. It is properly entitled *A Message from Arunachala*, because it was written in a few weeks at his saintly master's hermitage on the lower slopes of that hill. He has described this hill in the first chapter, wherein he shows what sacred and inspiring associations it possesses.

On two occasions I have visited the hill and the hermitage, and on the second occasion renewed my friendship with Mr. Brunton, watching the rapid addition of page after page of this work.

This volume is an application of the main

teaching of his revered Master, the Maharishee, who was mentioned in *A Search in Secret India*. This doctrine, namely, "Know Thyself," has been applied in principle to various problems of modern life. The final chapter gives the climax of his teaching, and transports us from our worldy surroundings to spiritual heights.

Incidentally I may mention that Arunachala is primarily the name of a hill, and not as the learned reviewer of *A Search in Secret India* in *The Times*, of London, seemed to think, the name of a person. The word in Sanskrit means "red hill," while Tiruvannamalai, the name of the township which nestles near its foot, means in Tamil "sacred red hill." It is a habit of people in India to name their children, not only after the names of a deity, but also after sacred places such as rivers, hills, etc. Thus we come to find in the south men bearing the name of Arunachala.

We Indians have lost much of our ancient spiritual and philosophic heritage. We have now to recover the basic gold that lies in it, cleansed from the dross in which it has become encrusted, under the inspiration of books like the latest one of Mr. Brunton.

In the faith that the readers of this book will find it not only equally interesting with his other works but perhaps more profitable spiritually,

I commend it to both the Eastern and Western world of readers. I hope it will be a link in bringing both hemispheres spiritually nearer to co-operate in the future evolution of a superior humanity.

CONTENTS

A MESSAGE FROM ARUNACHALA

CHAPTER I

THE HILL

Somewhere in South India there is a lonely hill which has been honoured with a high status in Hindu sacred tradition and legendary history. It lies near the same latitude as French-ruled Pondicherry, yet does not enjoy the latter's advantage of catching the cooling coastal breezes. A fierce sun daily flays it with darting rays. Its form is uncouth and ungainly—a tumbled, awkward thing whose sides are jagged and broken, whose face is a mass of jumbled rocks and thorny scrubs. Snakes, centipedes and scorpions lurk beneath the crevices of its multitudinous stones. During the dry summer months, cheetahs make their bold appearance with dusk, descending the hill in a snarling quest of water.

The whole peak offers no pretty panorama of regular outline, straight sides and balanced proportions, but rather the reverse. Even its base wanders aimlessly about on an eight-mile circuit, with several spurs and foothills, as though unable to make up its mind as to when it shall come to an end. Its substance is nothing but igneous and laterite rock.

A geologist friend from America who visited me lately proclaimed Arunachala to have been thrown up by the earth under the stress of some violent volcanic eruption in the dim ages before even the coal-bearing strata were formed.

In fact, he dated this rocky mass of granite back to the earliest epoch of the history of our planet's crust, that epoch which long preceded the vast sedimentary formations in which fossil records of plants and animals have been preserved. It existed long before gigantic saurians of the prehistoric world moved their ungainly forms through the primeval forests that covered our early earth. He went even further and made it contemporaneous with the formation of the very crust of the earth itself. Arunachala, he asserted, was almost as hoary and as ancient as our planetary home itself. It was indeed a remnant of the vanished continent of sunken Lemuria, of which the indigenous legends still keep a few memories.

The Tamil traditions not only speak of the vast antiquity of this and other hills, but assert that the Himalayas were not thrown up till later. Untold centuries, therefore, pressed their weight upon this time-defying pile which rose so abruptly from the plain.

And yet this unbeautiful and doddering grey-beard among heights took my heart in pawn a few years ago and would not let me redeem the pledge. It held me captive in an intangible and indefinable thrall. It imprisoned me from the first moment when my eyes glanced at it till the last reluctant turning away of the head. I could no longer regard myself as a free man when such invisible chains clanged around my feet.

Even when I thought, in the memorable year when the Overself stretched forth its hand to touch me, that return to the distant lands of the West, to the cold, grey, but vitalizing lands of the North, would save my health from the darkly shadowing clouds of physical prostration that loomed threateningly over me, I did not properly estimate the force of this attraction. Time crossed the ocean with me and made me feel once again stingingly cold January winds, chill February days, dark November fogs—in fact, all those elements in Europe's climate which, formerly, in my ignorance, I had detested. Then he took me hither and thither, but the triangular shadow of Arunachala fell constantly across my path.

I was not permitted to forget my distant captor. Again and again the question was flashed across space, as by some telepathic system of wireless: " When art thou returning, my truant one ? For thou canst in no wise escape me, *and thou knowest it !* "

Yes, I knew it. That peculiar glamour which invested the hill would prove too magnetic for me. And then, at long last, I had returned. Arunachala, the irresistible, had re-conquered me.

♣

I set out the other night to make the ascent to the summit. Night was a curious time to begin such an operation, but then, it was nevertheless the coolest—an important consideration in European eyes in a place where temperatures mount to fantastic degrees. I made my way through the deserted township streets to the western gate of the vast temple, which stood opposite a rough-hewn path. Priests and pilgrims took this path once every year and, when their slow climb was finished, lit an immense beacon on the hill-top. My own journey was but four days later than theirs and the yellow flare was still alive. It revealed itself fitfully under a heavy, milk-white mist that enshrouded the peak, which looked like a giant ghost in the starlight.

A full moon peered down from an indigo sky, illumining the huge structure that towered up over the gate. Two bats flew swiftly down and almost brushed my face. I rested in a wall niche, where I sat for a couple of minutes to gaze at the gaunt black silhouette before me, and to feel the serene peace of the night. A few trees dotted the scene, but the rest was rock and dust.

With a pocket torch picking out the ill-defined way, I moved upwards at last, climbing over the cactus-encircled granite rocks which Nature has scattered with a plentiful hand. I pushed onward as rapidly as I could, bent on reaching the top before the morning sun had waxed to fiercest power. The mists thinned into semi-transparent filmy veils and moved slowly around the peak, and with their passing the first grey light that preluded dawn showed itself in the east across the township, and touched the landscape's face when I looked around. Now and then a huge boulder of pink igneous rock bordered the path and bore on its sides the marks of a mason's chisel—evidence that the hill had been used as a quarry and had been chipped for material wherewith to construct the temple.

The entire gaunt hill-face soon took on a reddish appearance under the temporary transformation worked upon it by the waxing dawn. From this colouring had come its name, for Arunachala is but the Sanskrit word for "the Red Mount."

Stumbling a little, slipping sometimes, jumping occasionally across gaps, I put all my energy into making a speedy climb, and when the eastern sun had softly suffused the horizon with fiery red-coloured masses, a third of my task was at an end. Night had completely fled, the stars no longer inhabited the sky, day was fully in the ascendant, and I rested on the smooth top of a boulder to sip some tea and to gaze at the panorama spread out at the foot of the hill. The entire picture was enveloped in that yellow tropic light whioh gives such a scene its final splendour.

From this height one received an imposing view of the general plan of the temple, which was set amid straight streets and bazaars in the centre of the little township, and the latter again in the centre of a large flat plain. Nine lofty storied gate-towers, completely covered with a wealth of carved figures, rose in sculptured magnificence out of the square compound behind high enclosing walls. Did the gradually diminishing forms of those giant pagodas, with their broad bases and narrow tops, symbolically hint at some point in the sky where solid matter disappeared into infinite spirit? Did the aspiring structure of the temple, with its upward-pointing pagodas, offer a silent parable in stone? Their curious pyramidal shapes carried my thoughts back again to Egypt, to the land where similar towers could be seen over the old temple gates, but entirely bereft of these profuse and elaborate adornments. The Egyptian pylons possessed the same sloping sides, the same truncated tops, the same internal narrow stairways, although beyond that the resemblance stopped. The taste they betrayed was simpler and sterner, while the result was perhaps grander and more impressive. I meditated anew on the mysterious connection between ancient Egypt and pre-Aryan India and remembered the statement of a great Seer, the Maharishee, who lived at the foot of the hill, and who told me how the lost continent of Lemuria had once stretched all the way across the Indian Ocean, embracing Egypt, Abyssinia and South India in its confines.

I had seen signs a-plenty that the religion and society and monuments of the Dravidians in South India were derived from Lemuria, and that among those who settled on the Nile were their cousins or closer. Thus the culture of lost Lemuria was carried in a westward stream to mingle in Egypt with that of Atlantis, which disseminated its civilization to many a distant place in the Near East. The Lemurians first settled in Upper Egypt, while the Atlanteans overspread Lower Egypt, and hence the "Two Kingdoms" which endured so long before historic times saw their union.

♣

I listened to the dull beating of tom-toms that came from the temple and then turned my eyes to the west, where there stretched away the dry scrub jungle, green patches sparsely dotted with scattered brown rocks, occasional huge boulders of erratic shape, and barren tracks of gravel; the whole sustaining bare life to spiky cactus plants and barbed prickly nettle. It was officially marked in Government records as a Reserved Area of waste land, and was about three hundred square miles in extent. The whole jungle scene was wrapped in an aura of silence. That uncouth and mysterious plant, the savage-looking cactus, was ubiquitous and abounded in the region, so that wherever one looked grey-green spikes were thrust out in seeming defiance of the world. The wild cactus is one of those plants that seem to thrive in adverse circumstances. Snakes are particularly fond of its twisted roots. Down in the plain ground-nuts and rice, the two staple food products, were fitfully cultivated. The rice-fields, bordered by picturesque palms or heavy-loaded coconut trees, made vivid green islands in the surrounding sea of dusty brown.

Around the hill's base ran the circular road, its sides dotted by curious shrines and miniature temples, now worn down by the attrition of ages and half-crumbled to stones and dust. On the whole it was pretty countryside, with its slopes, trees, rocks and ponds.

The way led up the steep stony bed of a dried streamlet. A few caves were hollowed out of the side, and others were formed by nature out of huge piled boulders, their entrances sometimes screened by low tangled bushes. Once, these caves had been the natural cover for leopards and tigers, but now the latter had disappeared, leaving them empty or else tenanted by world-renouncing hermits and monks, who had turned away from the pleasures and comforts of life.

With my face turned upwards I continued the steep ascent. My shoes crunched the chips of rock against the red gravel as I climbed. And when at last I reached the strangely desolate summit itself, I sat down on a scorched boulder, clasped my hands around my knees, leaned against a pile of tumbled stones to rest, and contemplated the impressive scene around and below me. The light morning sun beat down on my unthatched poll, for I had a whim every now and then of wandering out without a sun-helmet, just to defy the sun's rays and to harden my resistance to them.

The temple was now but the size of a toy structure and the world which surrounded it had grown remote. I could sit comfortably apart from the planetary theatre which had been the scene of my operations for so many years. From this peak-top I could evaluate those activities and those persons in both East and West with whom I had been thrown into contact, but especially with those of the West.

I watched a huge vulture hover over me high in the sky, then swoop low, circle round, and finally perch itself on a square boulder by means of its ugly large claws. After some strident croaks it preened its feathers in a clumsy manner and showed its horrid bare red throat. On my left there was a huge black cauldron and around it were numerous emptied red earthenware pots which had contained the camphor and butter-fat used to feed the annual beacon, whose last flames were still burning smokily above the rim of the cauldron. For ancient tradition had dedicated this hill and its temple to the god Shiva, who had appeared upon the peak-top in the form of a spouting flame, and so custom had established the habit of lighting the beacon in annual remembrance of the event, which had ended the darkness that had formerly enveloped the world. Immense was the good fortune promised to the worshipper on the hill-top who beheld the first flame that leapt up out of the cauldron in the dark December night. I reflected that if I had missed such good fortune, at least I could satisfy myself that I was the last person to behold the dying flame that year. But I had already found my own good fortune and needed no other, for I had discovered long ago one of the last of India's spiritual supermen in his hermitage, which slept amid its coconut grove at the foot of the hill. He was none other than the mysterious Maharishee, the " Great Seer," the Illuminated Sage of Tiruvannamalai. I " sat at his feet," as the ancient Indian phrase for pupilship poetically terms it, and thereby learned, through a dynamic experience, of what divine and deathless stuff man is really made. What higher fortune than that can we pitiful mortals require ?

Half-way down the hill and somewhat to one side where a rivulet of cool, clean crystal water splashed out of a crevice in the burning rocks, there was a large natural cave where the Maharishee had lived, unknown and unnoticed, unrecognized and unappreciated, for a period of his young, ascetic, quietistic manhood. Year after year he must have stood there and gazed at the same panorama, aloofly watching humanity from this height, watching the world represented by yonder temple and township, which he had left. Three or four larger hermitages, each containing a few anchorites, were scattered about the hill.

In that gloomy cavern the Maharishee had spent uncounted hours of intense spiritual absorption in seraphic peace, locked within the folds of his own heart, where dwelt divinity. He sat as immobile as a rock in the ocean, cross-legged in meditation. We foolishly imagine that such a man has failed to keep up with the bustling procession of life. It never occurs to us that he may have far outstepped it.

The Sage once selected some verses from an ancient historical scripture of South India, which refers to this remarkable hill. This scripture, known as *The Skanda Purana*, is itself of immense antiquity; his chosen verses are here freely translated:

"That is the holy place! Arunachala is the most sacred of all! It is the heart of the world. Know it to be the secret and sacred heart-centre of the god Shiva! In that place he always abides as the glorious Mount Aruna.

"Shiva said: 'Though in fact fiery, the dull appearance of a hill on this spot is because of grace and loving solicitude for the spiritual uplift of the world. Here I always abide as the Perfect Being. Meditate then that in the Heart of the Hill surges the spiritual glory within which is contained all the worlds.

"'That whose sight suffices to remove all the sins which alone obstruct all living creatures from perceiving their true spiritual nature, is this glorious Arunachala.

"'What cannot be acquired without infinite pains—the true meaning of the scriptures' mystic revelation—is easily got by all who either directly gaze at this Hill or even concentrate their thoughts upon it, if afar.

"'I ordain that residence within a circle of thirty miles of this Hill shall alone suffice to burn off all defects and blend a man with the Supreme Spirit.'"

But one did not need to go so far back as this time-tattered book to discover the mystic repute of Arunachala. For the Maharishee has himself composed some short prose-poems of singular feeling and pathos, addressed to the Hill. I take a few verses at random and string them loosely together, to show what this wonderful Sage himself thinks of the rugged height.

" Why did you, entering my home and luring me to yours, keep me prisoner in your cavern ?

" Enticing me from my home, you stole into my heart and allured me to your abode. Oh, blazing column of Light in the shape of Arunachala Hill.

" O Arunachala, appearing as my Master and making me faultless and worthy, keep me in thy grace.

" In silence you communicated and commanded me to be silent ; and you kept quiet yourself. ' Look within ; gaze steady into the Self with the inner eye ; then it will be found '—thus you directed me.

" Did you not call me ? My well-being is now your burden.

" The very moment you welcomed me, entered into me, and vouchsafed divine life for me, I lost my own individuality.

" The Hill—enchanter of lives—entices one for having only once thought of it, makes him susceptible and eager for itself and as quiescent as itself ; lastly, preys on his soul made sweet by self-surrender. Beware of it, O men ! Such a transformer of lives is this magnificent Arunachala Hill.

" Hark ! Though looking inanimate and barren, this Hill can eradicate worldiness. Its doings are mysterious and past human understanding. From early childhood I had a vague understanding that the word Arunachala was sublime and unique, yet I could not penetrate its meaning. On being drawn to it unawares, on close contact I found it to be this Hill; then I stood motionless and understood that Arunachala was Perfect Repose."

Such were the thoughts and feelings aroused in this great Seer's heart and mind by this strange peak up whose rugged sides I had climbed. Moreover, the Sage has told me from time to time amazing tales of his psychic experiences in connection with the Hill. He has found it to be the abode of a host of spirits of varying grades, culminating in the spirits of great Sages, Perfect Beings who possess marvellous powers, and who arose and greeted him kindly when he first made their acquaintance. "Arunachala is a natural Pyramid," he had added, thus half-humorously referring to a somewhat similar experience of my own in the famous Great Pyramid of Egypt.

♣

Out in that modern world beyond this Lemurian height, that world where men give their passionate adherence both to deluding hopes and bitter necessities, there seethed an ocean of multitudinous activities whose nature varied from the gravest undertakings to which man had ever put his hand, to the gayest flirtings with well-bedecked pleasures that his fertile mind could hit upon. The truth was that they worshipped Matter. They loved material life so strongly that they had lost the feeling for the spiritual life which formed so dominant an element among the ancients. Out of that portentous loss had sprung all the troubles which threatened their social framework, their peace of mind, and even their continued existence. I knew that this slow-grown calamity was the root cause of every woe which had descended on mankind, because I, too, had once steeped myself in the very midst of that frail-based existence, and because I had now detached myself from it, therefore becoming possessed of a point of view which could alternately, and at will, take up a position either inside or outside that framework.

I knew the world and was not afraid of it, as some life-renouncing monk might be afraid of it, and could therefore judge it without bias. Here, on this rugged granite boulder, on this solitary hill-summit, on the sacred peak of Arunachala, I might view it and survey mankind once again, from afar, in the hope that the viewing mind might inscribe some tablets with a few thoughts which could, perchance, serve my fellow-mortals.

♣

The declining sun had begun to sink into its nightly home when I reached the foot of the hill again and entered my tiny twilight-shadowed cottage after a day spent at rest in the overwhelming heat which dried and parched one's throat, my arms loaded with a burden of written tablets which I had carried down from the summit. They were written rapidly, at the bidding of a strange Messenger who gazed at me commandingly and said : " Give ear, my son, take up your pen and write. Search deep within your mind for its most vital thoughts. Yet set down no word unless the fire enters into your heart and its message burns within you. For the hour approaches when your world shall meet itself, shall see its own face unveiled. This is the time of weighing all things in the balance, and those who bear the pen bear also a heavy responsibility. Stand with mankind at the cross-roads and point to the grave issues that are at stake. And then, when you have done that, finish with the highest wisdom you have learnt, remembering always that the inscrutable Angel of Fate faces the human race to-day with a challenging double-edged sword. Have no fear but write. So be it."

I did not even take a few minutes to watch the sublime tropical sunset, when coppery gold lay side by side with vivid opal in the heavens, so stirred was I that evening; although I love these beautiful mystical minutes when the day flies in defeat before the conquering dusk.

Not many days passed before it seemed to me that I must unburden myself of those charactered Mosaic tablets, those indictments and commandments which I had carried down from my strange Sinai. Try as I might, I could not piece them smoothly together; they seemed but detached fragments; and time pressed too heavily upon me to let me labour overlong upon the task of making them into a connected book. The world, therefore, must take them from my hands as fragmentarily as they were put into mine.

If this volume, then, is no systematic treatise, I can also claim indulgence because Nature has not given me the mechanical brain fit to turn out such work. These pages have caught only reflections of my moods and echoes of my meditations. I cannot pretend to the methodical manner of those who are able writers and whom I must, therefore, admire.

So I present these souvenirs of my last wanderings upon Arunachala, and submit them to the wizardry of the printing-room, where the ghosts of men's thoughts are materialized into solid leaden slugs of linotype! And I launch these thoughts upon the sea of present-day indifference to spirituality, knowing that somewhere a few havens exist waiting to receive them. For the few then, I have written, and out of the infinite shall come gentle breezes to waft these writings along the right routes better than I could ever do.

CHAPTER II

PREFATORY

I have no desire whatever to solve world problems, or to run after the solutions of social riddles which have left cleverer minds than mine dismayed. I do not know any glib, well-oiled scheme that will work like a perfect machine when applied to humanity's self-made problems, nor half of one, or even a quarter of one. But I possess a few ideas which I would like to toss into the brains of a few persons. That is all. But perhaps it is enough : did not Napoleon say : "If the principles are right, the details will take care of themselves." And if I cannot pretend that I carry in my jacket-pocket an infallible project for the salvation of stricken society, I can claim that I do carry in my head and heart the only lasting basis of such salvation. Those who want facts to justify the criticisms in the following pages will find few of them here. Any man with eyes in his head can get all the facts he will ever want, if only he will look around to the north, south, east and west.

♣

The philosopher who runs about the world looking for problems in order to solve them, will soon find his hands fairly full. I would prefer to leave all such matters to our intelligentsia and to confine myself to the single issue cf *WHAT IS MAN?* But sitting upon the summit of this distant hill, one enjoys a rare opportunity of surveying modern life from afar as a privileged spectator ; of taking an aerial view, as it were, while the trenchant bidding that has unexpectedly come to me to set down the thoughts which arise cannot be ignored.

♣

Those who do not wish to exert their minds a little had better not read this book. A mere glance at some of its statements will provoke them to the point of protest ; a further glance may provoke them to the point of thought—and that is an uncomfortable state which it is always better to avoid. Yet I would like a man to arrive at an opinion entirely his own, rather than to accept the mere reflection of other men's thoughts. I do not pretend to write for the intellectually infirm ; there are pens enough for them pouring out an endless drizzle of conventional sentiments.

Here is a book which demands some thinking from its readers. Those who require mental spoon-feeding had better beware its pages. Books of truth are but fingers pointing to the reality and indicating its direction. They are not balloons which carry you to the desired objective. A man who will approach these pages as they should be approached may conceivably pause at any time and say: "This book is helping me to think for myself, to see the old problems in a new way." Which, you will observe, is not the same as saying: "This book deals with the old problems in the only right way." I leave such modest claims to the multitude who are shouting out their wares in our modern Babel.

♣

My own temperament is such that I must have intellectual freedom. I am sceptical enough to take pleasure in consorting with the scientific freethinkers, but religious enough to move harmoniously among the pious. I am philosophical enough to smile at the self-sufficiencies of both science and religion. Independence is the pleasurable penalty of all this. I could fit into no organization, nor could any organization fit into my nature. Organization sooner or later puts bonds upon the soul and I could not tolerate that.

A society or an association undoubtedly provides the recognized vehicle for spreading any cause to-day. But I see no cause in the public eye vital enough to arouse my excessive enthusiasm. So I am content to work as a free-lance and to toss a few ideas towards an appreciative minority.

♣

Nor have I escaped from the time-stained sects and novel systems in order to entrap myself in one of my own making. Those who would imprison both myself and themselves in a set of doctrines waste their energies. I have no formal doctrine, no ready-made system of thought. There is no special philosophy I would take the pains to prove. All that I possess is an attitude towards life. It is not a mental attitude. It is rather a strange sense of the inner value of man. But before I found that attitude I had to find myself. Ralph Waldo Emerson once wrote down a paragraph in his private journal whose words echoed three thousand miles across the Atlantic waves deep into my own heart. "I have been writing and speaking what were once called novelties for twenty-five or thirty years, and have not now one disciple," he wrote. "Why? Not that what I said was not true; not that it has not found intelligent receivers; but because it did not go from any wish in me to bring men to me, but to themselves. I delight in driving them from me. This is my boast—that I have no school of followers. I should account it a measure of the impurity of insight, if it did not create independence."

Therefore, those who are content to have a halter thrown around their minds and to be blindly led along by some swift-scribbling author, are hereby warned to keep away! I have no desire to throw out the grappling-irons and hook other souls on to mine. I wish to pursue a path of fullest independence, and to extend towards other men a freedom equal to that which I would have them give me. I will influence men if I can, but only that they might discover themselves—and with that a timeless life that will fulfil their best hopes.

Nor will those who think it my ambition merely to add one more to the few millions of books in the British Museum rightly interpret my effort. If they imagine I want to join the mob of writers who send forth brilliantly polished epistles from their comfortable study-rooms, they are mistaken. Every paragraph I have written has come hot from the fire of my own heart: if it could not do that, I would not wish to write at all. I am neither a public entertainer nor a public instructor. I have a message for a few, and for their sake I write it. I have some thoughts to offer as a spur to their aspiring minds, as a solace to their burdened souls, and as a pointer for their own thinking. I cry out in the wilderness of spiritual stupidity around me, not because I believe that many will listen but because I believe that a few are searching for these words.

I do not desire to become understood by any except my own, nor do I propose to permit my body to become enmeshed in the jagged wheels of argument. No explanation will ever explain what you cannot understand.

This message can never be popular, with its criticism of our matter-worshipping standards and its gospel of quiet meditation. The under-brained will not appreciate its evaluation of life's experiences; the over-brained will despise its impalpable inspirations as a retrogression towards exploded religious superstition. It is therefore to be expected that the book will be burnt in the bitter fires of their double contempt. "Did I bring forth what is in my mind, could the age bear it?" queried a Persian poet. Whoever seeks to spread a transcendental doctrine such as this must expect the almost certain mockery of the mob. For the difficulty of comprehending his thought forms door and barrier to the masses, although it makes an easy "Open Sesame" to the understanding few. He will be under no illusion. He will understand perfectly that once the unfamiliar phenomenon of a mystic message applied to material affairs dares to raise its head among us, the usual onslaught of verbal brickbats will be provoked. Nevertheless, one or two intuition-possessing auditors may perchance bestow a bouquet. But then, if he is wise, he will seek neither to preach nor to convert. He will proffer his thoughts only to those who care for them and tender his message only to such as will give it kindly harbourage.

♣

Those, too, who shall look in these pages for that decorum which is presumed to benefit a scribbling philosopher, shall look in vain. I must refuse to wear the mask which convention politely offers me. Rather than put a cold face upon warm feelings, I prefer to drop out of the category of the Respectable Learned, and to be placed in a less-admired one. It is better to offend the strait-laced academics and their legion of followers in order to be myself than to attempt to please them and merely succeed in being a copy of someone else. These pages are not the product of a library-haunter's chair. They are penned by one who has worked hard, lived hard and suffered much. Books which are redolent of the library-lamp can never carry the force of books which are written out of the heart. I must write without reserve, because these thoughts burn with a fierce flame in my mind, and demand expression. If I reach at the benighted with a verbal rapier, aiming swift and scornful strokes, I do so but to wake them up and not to injure them. When I contemplate the conditions of so-called civilized life in our time, my pen, which normally glides obedient to the hand, leaps out of control like a thing bewitched and traces words glowing and destructive, saturated with the vitriol of satire.

♣

Sometimes I hesitate to confide these ardent thoughts to cold sheets of paper. I fear that the latter will not communicate the momentous stirring which moves me as I write. I fear to read the printed pages later, half-expecting a disappointment as deep as that of the young idealist who comes to the metropolis full of rosy hopes, only to find it a grim and heartless taskmaster.

♣

Whoever thinks these pages form a preachment is cordially invited to tear them up. I desire only to toss a few dearly bought ideas into the air: whoever wishes to catch one or two of them as they fall, is welcome. These words may easily be rejected by the scornful, but they will one day—whether in this decade or later—echo back to tingle in their ears. That day is fated, for life admits of no rest while we are troubled by ignorance. People who have never done any thinking upon life can hardly be expected to be satisfied with the explanations offered by those who have. Whether or not I have gathered a few grapes in wisdom's vineyard, I hope at least to stir the sluggish into thought. I care more to arouse thought than to convey it. Our streets are crowded with men who merely echo the thoughts of others. Perhaps these paradoxes of mystic thought will prod them out of their mental laziness. Though I am not deluded as to the value of this counsel to my contemporaries, I yet hope it will puzzle them to set their cerebral atoms at work! To challenge opinion and to call forth thought are therefore two of the aims of this book.

♣

Shall I be concerned that these thoughts find but a few followers and that I turn my pen vainly upon these themes? "Every new opinion, at its starting, is precisely in a minority of one. In one man's head alone, there it dwells as yet. One man alone of the whole world believes it," brusque

Carlyle proudly pointed out. I shall write exactly as I think, in words that may hit many, but perchance help a few. How can I ever hope to become a popular writer ? I care only to write about that truth which is called mystic because it is so plain. And this sort of truth is the most unpopular in the world. If my words call up in your heart no echo of the conviction which is in mine, vain were it to bid you follow in my wake. I can but let my book move among men and seek out its own.

If any think that there are some serene and confident paragraphs in this book, let them know that the thoughts which slipped so easily off my pen were truths learnt through slow years of paid-for experience. Wisdom is hard to learn but easy to forget. Writers who have lived through every line which they indite, who depend upon first-hand knowledge rather than on second-hand reading, distil the troubled years into peaceful wisdom. And yet, despite that, the quiet paragraphs are few. For the world is like a sick man, dragging his weary carcase around to his own discomfort and as a painful object-lesson to others. And so if my pen rushes on like a crusader in its attempt to set down deep-felt truths, who am I to bid it lose its passion ?

CHAPTER III

POLITICS

The politicians try to forget the fact of God, and the great messages of guidance and warning which have been delivered to mankind from time to time by His Prophets. There is something in that which makes them uncomfortable. God is too far from this globe to make His presence felt, is their silent implication. Society cannot be based on divine laws, they say deploringly, so we had better base it on the laws of the farmyard, the manger and the menagerie. Yet government without God has not succeeded in making man happy, despite its plentiful promises. It has, however, succeeded in producing nations of spiritual paupers. For the politician, carefully shutting his eyes to the deeper realities of life, juggles with externals. He must believe either that life has a political purpose or a divine one. If he accepts the first, then he must give his strength to support political partisanship ; if the latter, then he may pay tribute in time and energy to the deathless spirit.

Politics belongs to the superstructure of life, the foundation being the spiritual outlook, the attitude towards life of the people themselves. We are busily erecting a shrieking tower of Babel, but we have not bothered to inquire into the quality of our foundations. And the latter are admittedly defective. Without the creation of a new spiritual attitude, a fresh programme of inner values, we toil like foolish men. If you must build, then why not build something that will last? Get your foundations right, then you may confidently carry on with the upper storeys of your building. And no organized society can long endure without a spiritual basis, that is, a moral basis, a recognition of the value of your fellow-men. Without such a basis your building must, one day, topple over. Do not be deluded by temporary success. "Ha, then you are an impractical idealist!" declares a critic, eager to score a point. I reply: "Who are the impractical ones, the Europeans who built a society which crashed in a tremendous fratricidal war in 1914, the Americans who built a civilization which crashed financially in 1929, or we who want to build upon the foundations of goodwill, justice and truth? Do not be deluded by temporary success, I repeat, because the greater the superstructure which you erect on defective foundations, the greater will be its fall."

♣

We have substituted the feeble figure of Expediency for the strong form of Ethics; let us not complain, then, if our weakling falls and rolls in the dust. A host of political panaceas are held out to troubled nations as positive cure-alls, for men are born blind, nowadays. They accept the transient and superficial in place of the permanent and true. They cannot see that a spiritual renaissance is a necessary pre-condition of a happy restoration. Giving a man a vote, when he did not have one before, does not make him less blind. Without this higher principle we shall continue to gather the tart fruits of our folly.

♣

Unless a state is governed with goodwill, reason, spiritual courage and justice, it is not really governed at all. It merely possesses a set of parchments and papers called laws, not right government.

We may regard democracy as having been established when every private person fancies himself as being charged with the public business; when every bricklayer drops his trowel in order to give, with an airy gesture, the right solution of economic problems over which the best minds in the country have been unable to agree; when every clerk leans back in his office chair to dictate the proper foreign policy which the Government should adopt relative to a country he has never seen, and is never likely to see. The wise citizens of a country are not to be counted by the census returns which mark down the millions of its population.

You cannot legislate a nation into goodwill. Many burn their votive candles before Socialism; do they realize that Socialism must have goodwill at its core—goodwill to the rich no less than to the poor—if it is to succeed. Until each man practises such goodwill towards his fellows there can be no real Socialism. Life must grow from within to without, no less than from without to within. The man affects his environment as certainly as his environment affects him. As the hearts of men widen out to embrace their fellows, so will their political and economic institutions express this feeling. And then the outer world will keep pace with the inner life.

It is a self-evident fact that nowadays selfishness is no monopoly of one class, but has been more or less socialized. The cultural distance between Poplar and Park Lane may be a matter of forty or fifty miles; the physical distance between them is about four or five miles; but the spiritual distance has now wellnigh disappeared. The hundred and one ghosts of economic, social and political troubles will not be laid before people are purged of excessive selfishness and learn the value of mutual goodwill. Meanwhile politics separates man from man, class from class. The consciousness of their spiritual nature unites men. If we gave such energy and such time to ascertaining our spiritual nature as we give to politics, our troubles would melt away of their own accord. This is a truth as stupendous as the Himalayas, yet we ignore it.

Yet though I write so harshly of politics, because

it brings out some of the basest passions and worst prejudices of people, it is a necessary evil. Somebody must govern us, somebody must make arrangements that conduce to our mutual welfare. I am sorry for those who have this unwelcome task in our ill-starred age, the world being as it is. The politician has taken to a path strewn with disappointments, and the plants that grow beside his path carry the sharper thorns of abuse and ingratitude under every rose of position and power. He has undertaken an uncertain pursuit, stupefied by the incense of popular applause which he has inhaled. The same mob which throws bouquets at him one year may throw brickbats at him the next. The same people who sing : " For he's a jolly good fellow," may turn later and hoot him with cat-calls. The same crowd that clamours for a new Government has yet to learn that change is not synonymous with progress. Meanwhile, the politicians, a-horse upon their ambitions, climb the uncertain hill of empty fame and transient reward.

♣

The social and economic diseases of our day are more deep-seated than the masses and most of their leaders realize ; therefore, they need deep-sinking remedies. The troubles are primarily spiritual and can only be radically cured by spiritual means. We have been beguiled by political quack medicines. We thought, and still think, to find in them the marvellous cure-all which shall restore the human race to its lost happiness. Politics is the modern substitute for religion—but both to-day have gone astray. The feverish search for panaceas in every place but the right place is itself a sign and symptom of the rot which is at work to-day. Sincere but haggard-eyed reformers, selfish but eager-eyed politicians, and the selfless few who devote themselves to public work as a matter of service—all plough the arid sands of politics in the hope of feeding the soul-starved humanity during this critical, unique age. Many of our real troubles are likewise primarily psychological. The superficial politician thinks they are merely statistical. Their solution will be found by going to the hearts and minds of the people, and not alone to sterile theories.

Our age does not care for the promulgation of the most ancient doctrines—voiced by Krishna, Buddha, Jesus and Muhammed long ago—that regeneration of society is to be obtained by individual change of heart and never by multitude of debate.

♣

I have arrived at sight of the truth that to take

my place among the following of political parties—whether blue or red—is to do violence to the integrity of my understanding. Each has its contribution to make toward the common welfare, but each exacts a heavy price in narrow limitations from its followers. Rather than take sides, I prefer to take my leave! The gods bless no particular political parties but use them all. As the restraining Conservative, no less than the onward-leaping extremist, forces are needed at different times to adjust the affairs of a nation, or to fulfil the purpose of its good or evil destiny, so the parties representing those forces are temporarily permitted to pass into power. There have always been Conservatives. There have always been extremists. Egypt, Greece and Rome knew them no less than England, France and Russia knows them to-day. In every age they appear. It is only the names that differ.

♣

Yet though I have resolved to keep aloof from politics, and to adopt a strictly neutral attitude towards it, this is not a course I recommend to others.

It represents a matter of taste and temperament, and it arises because my interests lie in other directions. There is plenty of room in politics for the man who will enter with selfless motive, with ideals of pure service, with wisdom and spirituality to guide his feet and divine energy to act through his hands. Such men will shine out like bits of yellow gold in quartz; they can go far and do much—but where can we find them?

We are politician'd as we deserve!

We like ideals well enough for drawing-room discussions and tea-table talk, but we cannot bear to see someone start to put them into practice. We clap our hands at the brave rebel, well knowing that our later ridicule will cause him to revert to the Respectable and thus Convention will reclaim its own. We like to listen to the radical remarks of a free mind, but soon find a way wherewith to fetter him, for it would never do for everybody to practise what anyone may preach. So, waiting for an appropriate moment, we crush him with criticism and hang his name high up on the gibbet; thus furnishing a suitable example to foolish iconoclasts and inexperienced innovators whose honest but humourless minds imagined

alone will not do it, but the power of the Spirit will. The effect of mere words preached to others is likely to fade with their echo, but concentrated thoughts of dominion and endurance and wisdom, that have gained intense power in overcoming the mind's long-established error, radiate their strength and illumination to every other mind within the sphere of their influence.

The only worth-while reorganization of society will come when a spiritual change in man himself has spread its ripples from one end of the human race to the other; all other reforms are patch-work; they cannot endure and will pass, after a more or less brief life. Blind selfishness will continue while spiritual ignorance remains; they are both the roots of man's life, and the fruits of the tree must ever be the same—unhappiness, oppression, trouble, discontent and strife.

We look to the State for our salvation when all history and all experience prove that the path to happiness is lone and personal. The State is made up of individuals and each man can better both the thinking and behaviour of at least one citizen whom he so often overlooks, namely, himself. Let us realize this inescapable truth and place less faith in the big schemes of little politicians —however well-meaning—to save their peoples or reform their countries and let us understand that we can find a larger happiness for the world only when we shall find it in ourselves. It might be said with some veracity that we have reformers in plenty who wish to reform everyone but themselves.

♣

No amount of materialistic tinkering with the physical forms of society will remove the danger of destruction that awaits it, because Nature also has something to say in the matter. She may wipe out in one day what society has built up in one century. And Nature is not blind, unintelligent; she is the instrument of the gods of destiny. Yet the world's passion for revolt cannot be expected to die down again until the just causes for complaint have been removed from its path. But if it were wiser, it would place the task of restoring happier conditions into the hands of men who possess spiritual wisdom combined with initiative in action. Although democracy has been the inevitable swing from a deteriorated aristocracy, the only form of social government which can give permanent benefit to any society is that of divine autocracy, by which I do not mean priestly autocracy. And although such a form of government may seem as remote as any star, the fact is not to be gainsaid, that a single man of God-illumined mind, selfless heart and dynamic will is better able to serve a whole nation than any other. Inspired dictators are the world's need. But their inspiration must come from the kingdom of heaven, and their dictatorial ways should be such as to arouse love, and not hate, in the hearts of their peoples.

CHAPTER IV

BUSINESS

The old kings of history are giving way to the new kings of business. The slavery of feudalism is wellnigh over, only to be succeeded by the less-apparent slavery of industrialism. There are no visible bonds, of course, but they are there. The mechanized life of many workers becomes a tread-mill, and the modern gospel of glorifying the tread-mill is not an appealing one. Factory life is too often soulless labour, a dreary existence in a leaden atmosphere. The metallic monster of this Machine Age has brought many benefits, but exacted a heavy price for each one.

For if industrial civilization has produced material helps to living on a huge scale, we must not be blinded to the fact that it has also produced spiritual hindrances to living. In a number of cases its extension has meant the extinction of a finer life. Applied science claims to have liberated much of the energies of man: its achievements are colossal; we are the involuntary witnesses on every hand: but it has only touched physical man, not spiritual man. The price it demands is heavy indeed. The soul is still in chains, the heart of man is heavier than before, his mind more restless and more worried. Science utilized by Business continues putting mankind off with promissory notes on happiness. "Only a few more years and then the world will be full of wealth and half-empty of labour, and you shall see how great a wizard I am," is its reiterated promise. And we, poor dupes, are taken in, all forgetful of the fact that happiness can come principally from the Spirit, with science and business as accessories after the fact.

♣

The ruthless competition of commercialism lures the strong to exploit the weak. The mad scramble of modern industry debars the gentler souls who will not willingly leave their ideals of honesty, truth and justice at home when they catch the 8.35 train to town. The young man who wishes to achieve some degree of spiritual success thereby courts failure in the commercial world. Both mechanization and our present commercial condition encourage false standards of success. They make it easier for the cunning, the cheat, the plausible, and the greedy adventurer to have an advantage over honest and better-talented persons. The man who is self-pushing and self-advertising is more quickly successful than the talented man who does not push himself. We thus exist under a social scramble, not a social order, where to get something for nothing at the expense of your fellows, to trick others that you might make your thousands, is esteemed a laudable thing.

♣

Besieged by excessive materialistic activity, hammered at by the battering rams of mechanized industry and ill-used leisure, the soul sits in the citadel of man and starves. We need to simplify our civilization if we would save it, but the materialist says we must complicate it, while the revolutionist says we must shatter it ! Both do not see that it is a dubious benefit to enrich the material well-being of the people, when the very act of enrichment necessitates a stepping down in the scale of spiritual values. Insensate activity that drowns all fine thinking and keeps men endlessly busy doing something to the crust of this globe or to their transient bodies, is scarcely better than doing nothing at all. The feverish life of a large city, keen on so-called achievement and success, is still only half a life. Men bound to a completely mechanical activity such as this, become but half-men ; they are crippled by the very thing they have created. Those who work too much and earn too little can hardly be expected to have the adequate leisure and free mind for ennobling studies. Some imagine that to precipitate ourselves deeper into Matter via mechanization will promote the coming of happiness for man. We may judge only by results ; the result of a century and a half of such precipitation is that man's spiritual life is half paralysed. The beaten and broken remnants of men who haunt our large industrial cities form fit evidence of these results. How many in a great city like London have discovered such an existence to be intolerable and bought their bottle of poison or ascended the parapet of the Thames Embankment and splashed out of such a dismal world and its sorrows ? Industrialism, efficiency, more machinery, yes, they surely have their place, but beware that you do not industrialize man's soul almost out of existence ; that the noisy wheels of your machines do not whirr him completely away from the divinity within.

♣

The spectacle of industrial achievement is not

to be viewed by its present proportions alone, but also by its spiritual results. Let us see it not only from the standpoint of size, but likewise from the standpoint of man's soul. Men who have become cogs in its giant machine may not realize the harm which it has done them—unless they are deeply cogitating cogs !—may not realize how all that is serene and fine and beautiful and creative within themselves is slowly being crushed out by its merciless wheels. The man who spends his life at an automatic lathe, and does no other work, is no longer a full-grown man ; he is a part of the lathe. The so-called "division of labour"—a phrase almost Biblical to the economists—should really be called the "division of man," for it consists in splitting a human being into a quarter of what he really is. The decline and disappearance of the handicraftman is a case in point. A modern boot factory will have one man making eyelet holes for the laces, and nothing else. This is his work during all the years of his life. In former times, such a man made a complete boot by hand and so could contemplate his job with dignity and satisfaction. Now he has lost the outlet for his human creativeness, and therefore lost one of his principal paths to spiritual creativeness, freedom and happiness. His eagerness to earn his subsistence has blinded him to the spiritual result, and he is often unaware of the harm done him. He can no longer hitch his chariot to any star, but rather to a set of cog-wheels. The machine which should have helped him win a freer life is hurrying his soul into the grave. Once he was a creator, when he worked at a craft. Work was then a joyous expression of his soul, and thus became partly its own reward. To-day he merely has a job. Industry without a soul becomes brutality. Millions in the West to-day provide the sad spectacle of souls slain by excessive industrialism because they could not come to conceive of anything more real, more important, than their drab mechanical daily toil.

♣

Yet mechanical progress and scientific ingenuity can be made the servants of man's soul, and not its slayer. The Machine is written large in the horoscope of man and we cannot avoid it. We must needs accept its cold and steely hands and not turn cowardly back to the laborious past. We cannot and need not turn back the clock, but we can use the machine aright, finding a balanced, wise place for it, and not let it become a Frankenstein monster to devour us. Just the same we may accept and use the comforts and conveniences of modern civilized life, without letting *ourselves* be enslaved and used by them. The Machine is the miracle of this age, but it is a miracle we have worked a little too often; for it is beginning to run man, whereas man ought to run his machine. We need every bit of help we can get from it to lighten human labour, but we do not need to crush the spiritual balance of life in order to get it. We ought to use our purpose of material progress not as a fetter, but to free ourselves.

There are victories over self which give a man more satisfying and enduring rewards than all his victories in business. The most striking of commercial triumphs will sometimes trickle away and leave a disillusioned and disappointed victor, but the self-conquering sage has won the prize of everlasting peace. The disappointed magnate may have been busy controlling five thousand people at one time, when the Sage was busy controlling one person—himself. Mammon does not give its devotees the best of rewards. Not for all the money in the world would I die twenty years before my time, as many an American magnate imprisoned in his business has done, nor would I spend my old age drinking nothing more appetizing that hot water, as one millionaire does.

The man who mistakes roguery for success is sadly in error. He loses the respect of worth-while people, and what is worse—the protective enfoldment of his Overself. A day will surely come when, either in the still hours of the night with brain rebelliously throbbing and sleep far away, or in the mysterious after-death condition that parallels it, the faces of his victims will rise like spectres out of the darkness to confront and haunt him pitilessly. It is not only a late supper that will give him insomnia; it is also a late conscience! He has sold his self-respect and his honour. God pity him—this man who has traded his soul, his peaceful nights, for a heap of shekels, who takes a crooked road to affluence and deserts character on the way! His fine clothes and glistening diamonds will not charm his lost protection back again. He has accepted the common worship of a bulging bank-account, a thing the world holds dear because, quite truly, money is the second greatest power in the world. But on the other side of his account is written an invisible entry which represents what he has had to give in return for his worldly treasure. He has given his soul.

He has been deserted by the divine protector. There are spiritual processes that operate beyond our ken, and he exemplifies the paradox of ill-gotten wealth, that success in the world has meant failure in life. More than one behemoth of modern business has become a helpless infant when born into the world of "the dead." For man is immortal and the spark of his being is inextinguishable.

In the old days a man who conspired against the life of the king was hung, drawn and quartered. In these days a man who conspires against the life of the people by cornering all there is of a certain commodity and selling it at an exaggerated price becomes a baron in due course and receives consequential honour in social circles. His anti-social activity may have brought him huge sums, without giving any corresponding return or service to the community. All the criminals are not caught and confined to Dartmoor. Some escape to Park Lane and become honoured guests in society. The manufacturer who makes a fortune and acquires a peerage by supplying needed commodities can justly say that he has earned them, but the man who ruthlessly manipulates prices to serve his own ends entirely is nothing more than a pirate. If business were worked under the soul's light, such parasitic speculators would cease to find a foothold. The business man exists for the benefit of society, society does not exist for the benefit of the business man.

♣

The Golden Rule is being covered with dust The Rule of Gold is master.

♣

If we judge by appearances, the reign of God appears to have been supplanted by the reign of dollars and dimes.

♣

In a better age business will be nothing more than the art of human service. Success will be the inevitable reward for the best service. The present idea is "What can I sell you?"—a phrase which has gone around the world. The new idea will be "How can I serve you?" The prosperity of a man or firm will grow as his reputation for service grows. Fame will be the recognition of service, not of mere paid publicity.

♣

Advertising and salesmanship have their rightful

place in life, but in a better age they will recognize their responsibilities. The art of publicity will then not degenerate into the art of conscienceless puffery. Advertisements written in shrieking superlatives were better not written at all. All the post-war tricks of our New Chelsea transplanted to Fleet Street are doubtless necessary weapons in the armoury of the advertiser, but he need not run amok when firing them. Every time we open our newspapers and magazines, the advertising columns fling hand-grenades at our eyes in the form of shouting types which exhort us in declamatory tones to buy this and use that; which gush exuberantly over someone's pills; which, pitiably blatant and brainless, advise us that the secret of human happiness lies in taking someone else's salts. Advertisers would be better employed circulating their pretty, but irrelevant, printed pictures of seductive damsels rather than making statements which are neither true nor a credit to their intelligence. Thus they might continue to lure away the hard-earned money of the proletariat or to make the gilded classes part with their five-pound notes.

♣

Modern super-salesmanship is a vice when it

becomes nothing more than an attempt to sell a man something he does not need by putting hypnotic pressure upon him. The man who enters an office and tries to bludgeon its occupant mentally, because he wishes to enrich his own pocket rather than render a service, is not a salesman but a ruffian.

Money is a vital ingredient of modern life, but excessive worship of this ingredient, to the detriment of every true ideal, has produced a greedy age. Mammon holds the field of our world, raising his coarse hands to create a mirage before the minds of men. He is worshipped no less by the well-to-do than by the ill-to-do. The world offers complacent congratulations to every one of his devotees who succeeds in evoking a liberal response from his deity. It ignores the fact that when too much property accumulates in one man's hands he is accompanied by new dangers to his soul. Every pound becomes a bond which trusses him to the life of this world. He must walk the razor-edge path of inward renunciation if he is to escape safely. He must consider himself a kind of trustee, accountable to the gods of destiny for the right, wise and considerate use of his wealth. Even the richest landowner in the country will possess only six feet of earth when he dies!

♣

Nature's bounteous table is loaded with an abundance of good things, yet only a few hands can grasp them. The rest exist in the world with empty hands, perchance half-starved, certainly insufficiently equipped with the necessities of a decent livelihood. Millions of such beings—men, women and children with warm blood and sensitive nerves that feel pain—live dreary existences that can only be called "cribbed, cabinned and confined." Many sink unregarded by the wayside in the general scramble, or go to the wall in despair, because of the harsh operation of a heartless system. "Am I my brother's keeper?" is an ancient plaint, but every God-enlightened man has answered in the affirmative. For every God-enlightened man knows that the human race must eventually become one giant family, one universal brotherhood; he knows, too, that whatsoever we do unto others is—by the mysterious processes of unseen laws—done unto us in turn.

CHAPTER V

SOCIETY

Stupidity enters our drawing-rooms and cajoles us with the club of Convention. Ignorance follows, and throws its crude fetters around our hands and limbs. Solemnity makes an appearance, moving with starched and stiff gait, and poses as spirituality. Fashion rustles her gay silks, affecting an air of mystery as she perambulates on two legs. Men of the world uttering polite persiflage and flirting women with lilting laughs, long-winded Victorian-descended conversationalists and epigrammatic young "wise-crackers," noble-faced saints and rouge-faced strumpets, strong-jawed mandarins of modern business with steel-trap mouths and steel-drill eyes, platitudinous politicians and their satellites of chair-warming office-holders, middle-aged men scorched by the flames of war in their youth and authors doomed to dusty neglect, angels in human guise and devils in polished raiment, dogmatic materialists and bewildered mystics, soured cynics and sweet débutantes ; those born without silver spoons in their mouths and those whom fate and fortune have conspired to supply with such desirable articles, the noble and the notable, visitors from other lands, heavy Hollanders, sprightly Spaniards and astute Greeks—all these are announced by the butler in turn and help to make up the society of our day.

Social talk abounds with weary platitudes because it generally discusses the obvious : the weather, for instance, is the most talked-out topic in England, yet it is the one subject that will prove of perennial interest in the months between New Year's Day and Christmas Day every year. Our conversation slips thus easily into the shallow and superficial, because we prefer them to the profound. That, of course, is no crime because it is native to our constitutions ; and so our minds instinctively seek for what is plain and palpable when they search for a topic of discussion. We make, however, the facile mistake of perpetuating the self-evident by repeating it in regular daily doses to such an extent that it begins to become a colossal bore. When the kind of conversation which will carry a man farthest is that which deals with the deep subject of whether or not it is going to rain to-morrow, it is time to put in a protest. Our talk is but a bubble, mere froth and folly, and with all our words we say little. Our speech reveals the fleeting personality, but carries no hint of the true eternal man. He who would dare speak in an everyday *salon* as the Overself bid him, and not merely roll his tongue, would be treated to significant glances by some or to overt sneers by others.

♣

The world no longer seeks for its sanctions in the profound pages of the classics or in the crystal-clear sayings of a Christ; whoever would dare to quote a scrap of such wisdom in a fashionable drawing-room would be airily dismissed as a highbrow, if not a bore. As for the squalid and unfortunate slum, one does not expect it to know whether Plato was a Greek general in the last war or a living manufacturer of Greek cigarettes. Anyone, therefore, who is so foolish as to wish to quote from the ancient Wise must retire to remote places and quote them to the sparrows, or else write them on scraps of paper and tie his tags to the unresisting trees.

♣

It might be well to remember, what the modern

generation does not care to remember, that unless we live by Principle and guide our feet by some worth-while standard or exemplar, we are no longer men and women but merely animals blessed with cunning. O yes, we flirt with fashionable theories and play with the newest cult, but we embrace nothing. Our superficial souls seek no true love, but are content with occasional lightly lipped kisses obtained from promiscuous sources.

♣

Man was born for happiness, 'tis true, but he was not born for a ceaseless round of deadening pleasures. But whatever God intended man to be, a little thought will clearly show that he was never intended to sink completely into his physical senses. Life is not only a cup of pleasure to be drained, it is also a measure filled with righteous effort. One must pity these weak wanderers in terrestrial illusions from whom we expect a fresh folly each week, these pleasure-seekers who rotate through their useless gears, and rot the while in their inmost hearts. While they banquet to the tune of jazz-bands, there is a skeleton at the feast, for—— ?

♣

Character is so old-fashioned, nowadays. A

good conscience may help you to sleep well but, so they tell me, a good dose of chloral will do the same! The lure of a painted life fascinates the fashionable and their proletarian imitators. The riotous living of one section forms fit complement to the misery of the other. Man has slowly climbed the tree of life and left his tail behind, but even now he often looks downward. If the elemental passions of man were not oppressed by the elaborate restrictions which law and custom have built up around them, the world would provide a queer scene.

♣

I am somewhat ashamed to confess that I have not yet caught the contagion of this jazz age. It is a fashionable fever I know, to run through a course of hectic nights and haggard days. It is quite correct to fling overboard congealed conventions. With the latter aspiration I am fully in sympathy, but to throw away the few decent things along with the bad, which humanity has brought down through the ages, is like throwing away the baby with the soapy water. And to grub along in the gutter of uncontrolled desires when one might be breathing the clean air of spiritual peace is likewise a form of folly. Many among the younger generation are materialistic to the finger-tips and pagan to the soles of their jazzing feet; they spend their leisure seeking some new sensation, some new thrill, repeating the daily dose of nerve titillation until it becomes an imperative habit, and finally a craving. This is hardly genuine gaiety. And so, that which rightly used might conduce to their true happiness —leisure—becomes poison to their souls.

♣

The world is snobbish. It truckles to a coronet, vaunts Mister Moneybags, but disdains a poor sage. Climbers seek to scale the pyramid of contemporary society, never dreaming that it might not be worth the trouble. The accurate crease of one's trousers is deemed more important than the accurate nature of one's principles. The mob, whether gilded or plain, is weak, and accepts the selfish fatuity of wealth and fashion as a thing to be highly prized, slavishly imitated and ardently aspired to. The elegant and mannered, who are more attentive to the cut of their clothes than to the thoughts of their hearts, accept the cash standard which is the criterion of present-day pseudo-aristocracy, whereas the true aristocrats will ever prefer to pay court to the obligations imposed upon character by high birth. The cumbersome apparatus of social privilege cannot deceive the clear-sighted, who realize that the wealthy and the titled, the powerful and the prominent, are worthy of respect only in the degree that their character deserves it—no more. Both prince and prelate are to be measured by worth—not by birth. I have nothing but respect and admiration for those aristocrats who inherit something more than a title and estate—and it has been my pleasure and good fortune to meet not a few of these, but I have neither respect nor admiration for those who have never learnt, and consequently never practised the virtues collected together in the words "*noblesse oblige.*"

♣

Though we have all bid adieu to a stiff and formal age in our new-found post-war freedom, this is not to say that we must also bid adieu to the spirit of considerateness and the quality of refinement. The vulgarian who puts on evening dress does not thereby cover his vulgarity, which still remains patent to those who do not rate a man's value by the methods of his bank manager. It is a deplorable fact that many among modern youth seem to have reached the tail-end of fine manners and dignity. If an early-Victorian were to arise from the grave and be granted a peep at the modern show, he would draw back with startled unbelieving eyes. It is true that the young have found nothing to admire and little to cherish in the institutions that surround them, and so fling our tame conventions aside and give their jazz morals free play, but when they say they want more liberty they really mean they want more licence. Though they may wear the finest clothes they have also to wear the finest manners, and to remember that considerateness for others and a measure of self-control provide the signs whereby we may discern true gentlemen. How many of the selfish young could appreciate the spirit of that gallant Elizabethan knight Sir Philip Sidney, who, at the battle of Zutphen, handed his only cup of water to a wounded soldier, although himself suffering the thirst-agony of approaching death. To take the rights and privileges of an honoured rank but to forget the duties that accompany them is nothing admirable.

♣

And yet the polished phrases of polite society are a poor substitute for the fact that many of the persons who are compelled to utter them are inwardly unhappy. Unhappy hearts reveal themselves to the discerning. The torments within themselves are not to be stilled by a multitude of dances, feasts and entertainments. It is one of the lessons they learn rather late that most of the attractive roses of life are painfully prickly with unexpected thorns. The ritual of society's unending whirl demands that they shall speak, not the words of their hearts, but the words of hollow sound. They are tortured by restlessness and know neither calm nor content. The young have lost all anchorage and simply drift upon the sea of stray emotions; while their elders have suffered from the hands of Time, the menacing thief who has stolen their youthful illusions and robbed them of early hopes. And so a secret melancholy hides behind each of their smiles. The faces which they turn to the world are not the same faces which they turn towards their own thoughts and desires in the lonely moments of sleeplessness.

♣

I see the authentic signature of spiritual decadence legibly written across society, whether that of Mayfair or of the slum, yet I entertain a great hope. I can say, with Abraham Lincoln: "And this too shall pass."

♣

After all, the best aristocracy is that of the soul.

A man is great, not because he was born into an exalted rank but because he was born with an exalted soul. All other aristocracies, however ancient and vaunted, are secondary. Jesus, for instance, was such a man. I am not aware that He met "the right people" and moved in the best society. If I remember aright these were the very circles who rejected Him. He mixed with the "wrong people" and the worse society. Perhaps that was because His love was so wide that He preferred the unloved to those who loved themselves. There was one among His disciples who denied Him through fear of the worldly authorities; let us not deny the Christ-self within us for fear of the conventional society into which birth has flung us.

♣

We spend our days occupied with the complicated art of fitting in with other people's opinion; we forget to BE. The judgment of the world holds us enchanted as by a magic spell, and we are afraid to break the chains in order to live our own lives. Even the so-called young convention-breakers of society need no courage for that because they do it *en masse*, and because they are merely yielding to uncontrolled emotion. We that the world would accept the road merely because it looked at the sign-post.

♣

I disdain political methods—although driven by expediency to accept them—because I rely on spiritual ones. As soon as you solve one problem by a political method, another will inevitably arise in its place. There is, there can be, no end to such troubles because the root—man's greedy warring nature—remains untouched. It springs up like a weed into new growths. Brains can plan improvements, but only goodwill can initiate them. There is only one way to deal with these problems that is really satisfactory and lasting. Change men, and you thereby change all the problems which arise out of their defective nature. This is a truth which will be repeated and remembered long after this era is gone. Spiritualize them, and in the atmosphere of goodwill which shall then arise you will solve all problems for good. For in the sublime atmosphere of the higher life, all troubles, frictions, hatreds and so on will vanish of their own discord, automatically. There will be no need to hack at the root of each separate one. But remember—you can begin to change men only after you have changed yourself. Words trim down or temporize our talk, because we fear to speak the truth straight from the heart. He that overcometh convention shall inherit his own soul.

The attainment of true happiness by the process of increasing his material wants is the absurdly Sisyphean task which man has imposed upon himself to-day. The complexities of modern life only hinder him from finding the true goal and distract his attention from looking within for satisfaction. The values of life are mistakenly assessed by one-sided standards, resulting in ironic and mocking consequences to society. The subordinate has become the supreme. There is a mania of restlessness in modern society. Men and women find no happiness except in incessant activity and endless excitement. We search the fields for food but pick up only straw and stubble, rejecting the real wheat.

Thus society clings to the circumference of the wheel of life and permits itself to be whirled and dragged on to it knows not what. But there are a few who have wrenched themselves away and stand before the Whirler of the Wheel with thought-tortured faces, demanding to know whither they are being driven. And unto them, sooner or later, there comes an answer. And then they find a new and passionate purpose in life; they gather some rare fruit from their days and not merely a heap of ash. From among the foremost representatives of modern science down to the humblest toiler in many a quiet farm men are yet to be found who cling to the vision that has been bestowed upon them, who do not doubt that the soul is divine and immortal, and who hold firmly to the ideals that their vision demands.

CHAPTER VI

WORLD CRISIS

The world has walked right into the greatest transition recorded in history, but the road it will tread thereafter is not easily discernible. Peacefully, by the light of reason, or painfully, by the force of circumstances, it will have to take a new orientation. That, the world realizes, but whither it shall turn it does not know. It is only at such a time, when many of the economic, social, political and religious values of national life have weakened, that men discover how feeble have been their supports, how uncertain their guides. Who can blame them for viewing the future with some misgivings? The ship has begun to drift, and few seem to know in which direction it is floating. This tumultous time in which we live is a dark and inexplicable hieroglyph, and hope is the one luxury left to us in our moments of foreboding. The gods can afford to wait their destined moment, knowing that it will change the situation completely.

Mankind's present state is aptly put by Scottish Burns: "And forward though I canna see, I guess and fear." That this planet and its people have been thrown into some kind of melting-pot since the vast conflict which staggered it in 1914 is fairly evident to every thinking individual who inhabits it. We were proud with twentieth-century pride of "progress"; then we were humbled and brought low. Our train ran moderately well in those days, although the wheels creaked loudly now and then—until one fateful August afternoon which many will never forget, when the town-dwellers were astounded by the hoarse cries of news-boys shouting: "War declared!" The common people knew little of a coming war, and it burst upon them like a bombshell. The birth of every war is the death of every hope. Only the few—secret service men with ears to the ground, helpless political leaders sitting in cold-walled offices and pulling wires which plunged the world in doom, rulers who were unable to rule themselves, and caused their nations to suffer through their weaknesses—only these had played with thoughts of war and prepared for it. And then the curtain suddenly rose and the first grim act struck all with terror, even startling the actors themselves. So we saw the blood-stained scenes and agonizing acts of the greatest drama which the Theatre of History had yet presented to mankind, a drama which reached its inevitable climax and final denouement only after a screen of fire passed across the planet, forcing all to endure its pitiless heat. Many were seen no more, others were left with grievous wounds, but all were shown the terrible Nemesis that had been brooding over the race of man. The world turned its back to God and its face to Mars ; it could not rightly complain when it was handed the bitter fruits of its choice. Yet it paid Mars a heavy price for the privilege of slaughtering fellow-beings, the while its deity chuckled over its stupidity for falling such an easy victim. The human carnage was unparalleled. Sammael, the Death-Angel, walked this globe from dawn till dawn and sat in the hall of the House of Man. During those slow bitter years, terror was master of the world. The bravest face had to blanch, for what mortal courage availed against the fiendish fruits of scientific ingenuity. Man could fight against man, but he could not fight against the awful array of hell's machines, against the murderous mechanical contraptions devised by his intellect. Mars hammered his pitiless blows down on his victim, gloating over the blood and tears, and raised pyramids of skulls as monuments to the lack of goodwill among humans. The bubble of Progress burst, and we saw that the materialistic strides we had taken drew their inspiration from the spawn of Minotaus and Circe, who people the darkness of perdition.

♣

After the war tempest had hurled its way across the planet and done its worst, did mankind lie like a prostrate penitent at the feet of the gods? Did we return to a truer life by the pathway of a voluntary *volte-face?* Did the world, sick of the glamour of war, find the less obvious glamour of peace? With the old civilization broken to pieces by the guns of war, did it organize a new and worthy one? Although it had reached a crucial epoch in history, a time like unto nothing that had gone before, a confusion and a chaos that offered the opportunity of making a fresh start, it soon slipped back into the old prejudices, the old futile paths, the old blunders. But it was too enervated for war, too tired to blunder into another red inferno, and so it blundered into the grey wilderness of economic chaos instead. The finer post-war state, which optimists of Press and politics predicted so glowingly, failed to make an appearance. Millions of people wandered the world seeking with ravenous eyes for a chance to work, a chance to gain bread and stave off the grim spectre of hunger. Millions more had work but had their minds slowly eaten away by the worries and cares of attempting to support families on wages fit only to support a man. The loathsome figure of Disease stalked into the crowds and added to their wretchedness. All craved for happiness but few found it. All became restless, nervous, eager, striving, strained and peaceless. It might be said that the age which came to an end in the early days of August, 1914, was at least an age more secure, more stable and in some ways more satisfactory than the age which had taken its place. At least one could wake up each morning reasonably sure that the world would not come tumbling about our ears in ruins, a surety none of us possess to-day. And so, with discontented hearts and unsatisfied minds, the troubled currents of our lives struggle on. We must both cry and laugh over the swift-moving drama of our days: so swift that no one seems to know what the morrow may bring forth, and so moving that none knows whether the direction be paradise or perdition. The world lives to-day a kind of rapid-motion picture reel, where event follows event in breathless sequence. Hardly anyone knows what the next scene will be like nor what the final climax is likely to be.

There was, of course, a very brief and very joyous period, ironically called one of "reconstruction," immediately after the war, when everyone said that such a dreadful conflict could and would never happen again, that it would be the last which our scribes of history would have to record. Our leaders and guides and others who sit in the high places declared—and no doubt quite sincerely—that the war had dug a deep moat around the past; henceforth we were to have a New Age wherein the dreams of political idealists and the aspirations of common people would find expression. One is surprised that no one thought at the time of destroying the old calendars and starting this promising pregnant period as the Year One. Many years have now passed by. With each year our hopes have receded. To-day no one hugs the foolish and futile illusion that we are living in a New Age, because we still see all the signs that indicate the presence of Mars in our midst. The victory of the last conflict turned out to be a hollow piece of vanity. Europe itself is mocked by a military peace, a strange state of volatile security. A glance at the international state of the world and the internal state of the nations shows that there is sufficient explosive material to warrant no rest, but rather restlessness. We read, like clairvoyants, the terrible tokens which Mars has cast anew in tangled cypher into the crystal glass of our world's future. We have a vague hope that some startling but kindly godsend will turn up an hour or so before it is too late, although this cloudy optimism is hardly warranted by the reading of history. A few are foolish enough even to regard the present state of affairs as blessed by God, canonized and sanctified, and not as a return to darkness; let us pity them for their blindness. Ours is a prosaic and practical people. Imagination is not one of our best gifts. But it does not need a titanic imagination to see the inevitable outcome of present conditions, if the world lacks the faith and courage to make a fresh start.

♣

How, then, did this error on the part of our optimistic statesmen come about? They expected so much; we find so little. They saw a new world; we perceive only the old world. The answer is obscure merely because we persist in looking in the wrong place for it. We blame this man or that man, this party, this race or that race, new conditions and old conditions—everything in fact but the real culprit. If you want the true answer, do not go to the statesmen, do not go to the business man, do not go to the fashionable men of the world, do not go even to the peasant working in his field. Go, if you can find them, to the Seer and to the Sage.

The Sage has all but disappeared from modern existence; we have no place for such useless foolishness as he is wont to practise. We want only busy, active, useful do-something men. But in ancient times there was always a place for the Wise Men. Jesus and Buddha are but two of the better known names among them of those days, and there have been a few others. Seers of this kind speak to us in authentic tones, use the universal language of divine inspiration, and shed grace on our hearts. A few—a very few—are still to be found in the East, because the East is still old-fashioned enough to find a place in its scale of values for such men. It is true that nowadays the genuine Oriental Sages "close the door" to outsiders who lack sympathy, while those who approach carrying the barbed arrows of hostile criticism get nothing for their pains, for they come away with false notions. But such Sages value what they have found too highly to display it before those who are unlikely to place a similar valuation upon it. And it is because they have stood apart from the broad stream of humanity that they are able to see what all the fuss is about. Their spiritual distance has given them perspective. The throbbing events going on in the world to-day are too close to us and do not readily surrender to our scrutiny. We do not perceive how pregnant they are with meaning for our future direction. We cannot read their deepest meaning, but the illumined Sage may, for he is watching from outside the field the game we play. He is a detached, impartial, percipient observer. He can see clearly what we can see but dimly. It is not that he indulges in the luxury of Olympian detachment and relapses into owlish silence while his fellows are overwhelmed by the stress of modern living; it is rather that he has learnt all the *essential* lessons which the school of such existence offers, and he has graduated with spiritual honours. He has no axe to grind and will tell you his opinion without personal considerations. He is free, fearless and truthful in expressing himself. Ask him, then.

♣

I have tracked down three or four such men and all agree in giving the same answer. Because, at the moment, I am living here in a tiny cottage at the foot of Arunachala, it is fitting that I give the statement which the Maharishee, the Sage of Arunachala, made not long ago when someone raised this hoary-headed query of distressful world conditions in his presence. The Maharishee, like most Sages, does not deliver lectures. His speech is terse and concentrated, and so his statement was short to the point of brusqueness. The Maharishee said: " Suffering turns men towards their Creator." Six simple words—yet what a whole philosophy is congealed within the phrase. You may think them platitudinous, and they would be did they not derive from a man who knew what he was talking about because he had ascended to spiritual regions beyond our ken, to regions where God *is*. Think them over and you will realize that they supply the reason why our optimistic statesmen made their error and why the world slips back into strife and war. For our leaders and the led should have profited by the terrible lesson of the last war and " turned towards their Creator." But did they? The present state of affairs is visible evidence for the negative. In all their planning for so-called " reconstruction " they omitted the one factor needful, the one vital factor that would award success or failure to their plans—they failed to turn towards their Creator. The tremendous suffering involved in the conflict had not cut deeply enough to provide this new orientation; the lesson had been very badly learnt. While they filled their heads with grandiose fantasies, the omission of the *x*-factor, of spiritual values, hurled their plans towards downfall and death even at the moment of their birth. Are we to repeat the suffering and learn the dreadful lesson in a severer form? Nature is always teaching us, but we are not always willing to learn.

♣

It would be a pity if we had to grope our way through a second world-war in order to find the looked-for new age of better things, but the fault would be our own. However, I am not of those pessimistic and morbid persons who regard such a dreadful happening as fore-ordained, and I venture to entertain a certain hope which may be denied to others. But it is fairly clear that unless something new appears in our midst to revive the dying spiritual life of the world existence will become a fierce jungle and life itself will lose its finer values. Although I am no croaking pessimist, although I believe that the innate heart of man is fine and sound, I am not blind to the menacing forces which are gathering around us. If the gods permitted the present materialism to go on indefinitely, within two or three more generations people would be studying the dictionary to discover the meaning of such terms as "spirituality, goodwill, kindliness, peace and unselfishness." We have wandered away from the track of spirituality; we must necessarily return. To continue farther from sheer force of habit and tradition is folly. Get back to the right road—such is the counsel dictated by wisdom.

♣

The gods are driving the world in a corner. Our so-called progress, our apparent upward movement towards perfection, turns out to be more and more one-sided and therefore illusory. Everything around us is thus a vociferous witness to the mistake we have made in cleaving the spiritual core out of life. We are progressing into a cul-de-sac. Defeated Nature has exacted her revenge in other ways. Every improvement in material life has been paid for by mankind with bitter price, with loss of spiritual insight and psychic faculty. If the world is wise, it will frankly recognize the position, submit and surrender. A hundred remedies have been offered to our decrepit civilization, from raging revolution up to complete dictatorship, but the illness is such as to defy all remedies other than those based on a recognition of spiritual values. A spiritual sickness needs a related remedy. The vision of God in man which upheld great leaders of the past and brought great deeds to birth, is gone. Unless it is restored, all our efforts must continue to prove painfully futile. Those only who can restore that vision have the right remedy. We have put last things first, and first things last. This is the chief reason why mankind is in such a bewildered chaotic state to-day, why the world is sick at heart with its woes. The political, social and economic problems are but a heavenly built façade which hides the real problem. It is man's wrong attitude towards life—and hence towards his fellows—which forms our major trouble. If that could be put right, everything else would automatically be put right. Men argue fiercely about their Governments, but miss the true cause of all their troubles—themselves! The disillusioning experience of the post-war years indicates that mankind has not faced its crisis in the requisite spirit. Wrong modes of thinking must be discarded. The world cannot evade the issue. It must accept the Golden Rule—or accept defeat. We must not take near-sighted views. A nation which is willing to be guided by higher principles is bound to benefit in the long run, whatever the worldly-wise may say. The task of spiritualizing our values, the work of under-pinning our civilization with diviner materials, cannot fail to justify itself completely.

♣

For man cannot be without a higher life. Russia deposed God only to deify Communism. Man may pretend to be indifferent to the thought of God ; he may even boldly declare himself a downright infidel ; nevertheless there is a lurking uncertainty as to whether he is right. Thus, even in this way, God is trying to speak to him. Is it to be expected that the gods will permit the millions of this world to perish miserably, their last hopes carried to burial, bereft of spiritual light and sunk in the stupor of material existence ? We who believe in the reality of that Higher Power think not ; we await the appointed hour of destiny when, within easily measurable time, the dimmed lamp shall shine anew. Then man, purified by suffering and illuminated by higher experience, shall rise again from his low state and resume his divine sovereignty once more.

CHAPTER VII

RELIGION

The mass intelligence is in pitiable arrears of the findings of advanced scientists like Einstein, Eddington, Lodge and Jeans. While the former has been sinking deeper into material consciousness, the latter have been rising up into confirmatory contact with the truth of spiritual reality. Science, indeed, through its best minds, has become a little more reverent. Yet it has not to thank the doctrines of religion for its advance, it has to thank its own sincere efforts. Religion, which in ancient times instructed men in truth and gave them vital spiritual sustenance, broke down before the developing intellect of man and could not meet his reasonable criticisms. If the doctrines which in their mixture pass as religion to-day had been one hundred per cent true, religious leaders would have had nothing to fear from the progress of science.

The Scientist has begun to strip away the

disguise of this universe, and to scent the presence of its Creator.

I am not a member of any religious faith, in the conventional sense, not a Christian, Jew, Muslim or Hindu. And I will frankly confess here that I was born with no particular leaning towards religion—while the splitting of theological hairs aroused my amusement. But I am a believer in most of the great faiths according to the interpretation which, I hold, their own Founders gave to them. I am a Christian to the extent that I concur with Saint Paul in saying: "And if I have the gift of prophecy, and know all mysteries and all knowledge, and have not love, I am nothing." I am a Buddhist to the extent that I realize with Gautama, that only when a man forsakes all his desires is he really free. I am a Jew to the extent that I believe profoundly in the saying: "Hear, O Israel, the Lord our God is One." I am a Hindu to the extent of believing and practising the kingly science of yoga, the science of union with the spiritual self. I am a Muhammedan to the extent that I rely on Allah above all else. And finally, I am a follower of Lao-Tse to the extent that I accept his perception of the strange paradoxes of life. But I will go no further into these faiths than the points indicated ; they are the boundary-posts at which I turn back. I will not walk with Christians into an exaltation of Jesus—whom I love more deeply than many of them—over the other messengers of God. I will not walk with Buddhists into a denial of the beauty and pleasure which existence holds for me. I will not walk with Jews into a narrow shackling of the mind to superficial observances. I will not walk with the Hindu into a supine fatalism which denies the innate divine strength in man. I will not walk with the Muhammedans into the prison house of a single book, no matter how sacred it be. And finally, I will not walk with the Chinese Tao-ists into a system of superstitious mummery which mocks the great man it is supposed to honour. I do not believe that God has given a monopoly of Truth to any of us ; the sun is for all alike. No land or race can claim a monopoly of Truth, and the divine afflatus may descend on men everywhere. No creed has the power to copyright Truth. Therefore I can take a detached and impartial view of them all. I can perceive why they rose to greatness, and why they are, in some cases, in their decline and fall.

♣

Each creed and sect fondly imagines that the

Creator takes a special interest in its particular affairs. Commonplace everyday happenings become transfigured through its rose-spectacled gaze into special dispensations of God! The pettiest events loom up as remarkable miracles performed on its especial behalf. It needs to keep a sense of proportion in these things.

♣

The denominational differences which caused the Puseyite of forgotten memory to deny heaven to the Presbyterian, and which deluded the Presbyterian to close its gates to the Puseyite, have fallen away into futility in this rational age. The futile wranglings of our sects must die away abashed before the Great Presence. Said the Persian prophet, Abdul Baha: "Religion should unite men everywhere; instead it sunders and separates them. Religion has proved a razor among men, when it should have healed all their wounds." Thinking men observe this and lose their ardour for that which should give man his ardent support. It is an illuminating and instructive commentary on modern life to note that a lecturer at University College, London, asked his students two questions a few years ago. "Do you believe in God?" was the first; the answer was a unanimous "No!"

"Do you feel any need to believe in God?" The second answer was a nearly unanimous negative. Can we entirely blame those young undergraduates? Many theological doctrines now smell of the cemetery; their decaying bones repel the virile young crowd of our century. Thus, coded religion in most parts of the world has long passed the June of its life and is beginning to show the shrivelled form which precedes decay. The dark ages of theological thunder, when people were brought to the feet of a fabricated God through sheer fright, are no more.

♣

Although we have begun to doubt religion so devastatingly, it is not necessary to throw away the baby with the soapy water! Although we are busy rejecting the superstitions, absurdities and bigotries of religion, it is not necessary to throw away its beauties, truths and inward realities.

♣

When the creeds creep in and set up the wooden idols, then spirituality heaves a sad sigh—and departs. From the straight and narrow path shown to men by Jesus, we are confronted to-day by three hundred broad roads. Each is termed Christian ; each is supposed to lead to Heaven.

It is convenient for many to remember Christ's birthday every year, but just as convenient to forget His principles.

Theologians disagree and differ. To understand how simple and sweet-tasting spiritual truth can be, we need only to read the sayings of Jesus ; to understand how tortuous and repulsive the unillumined can make it, we have but to read the wretched effusions of some who preach in His name. To know with what kindness the spiritually strong treat the spiritually weak, we need but to remember how Jesus spoke to Mary Magdalene ; to know with what cruelty the pseudo-religious will crucify human frailty, we have but to learn the inner history of every town in Christendom. God is a subject men often talk about but rarely understand. As I read through the red pages of history I cannot trace many of those soft deeds of mercy which Jesus taught His followers to practise. Yet every hamlet in Europe has its church, and its church bell clanging the call to the devout. Precisely the same thing has happened in India under another faith. Stolid clerics and purblind priests, whose hearts are more full of dead doctrines than of divine love, should not blame science, sceptics, modernism or materialism for the falling away of followers, but themselves.

♣

Such is the kindness of some clergymen that if they bore us with uninspired sermons when we are alive, they comfort us with consecrated graves when we are dead. Listening to the lifeless sermons of some clerics it is hard to believe that they really feel what they teach and have confidence in what they preach. It is hard to believe that they, too, have been converted with Saul on the road to Damascus, or stood with Jesus fearlessly before Pilate.

♣

They seem to be men who have become excessively Bible-bound, narrowing life down to a matter of script and quote, unable to confirm by their own experience the high teaching they attempt to propagate. And with their worldly wisdom they have shorn the sayings of Jesus and Krishna of their true meanings and implicits.

Once, the priest interpreted God to man; now he interposes himself between God and man. The temple priest in India is first cousin to the church priest or clergyman in Europe. The tale of most religions to-day is the same; uninspired priests rule in the places where once inspired prophets lived. Our disillusioned century has made the unpleasant discovery that its spiritual guides are not necessarily spiritual; that when they bless opposing armies or propound contradictory policies with equal vehemence, they merely reveal themselves as ordinary blind men who hold opinions, just as you and I and other lesser mortals hold them. And it is also true that the custodians of sectarian religion in every land were among the first to attack true Religion when the latter publicly appeared and was voiced by the great Prophets. As they drew their stipends for supporting a mixture of lingering obsolescent superstitions and hardy truths, it was hardly to be expected that they would support undiluted Truth.

♣

Any jerry-built villa can be more sacred to you than Jerusalem, provided you think sacred thoughts when you live in it. True holiness is within ourselves, not in stone walls and timbered roofs.

♣

Five different religions are simply five different ways of talking about the same God.

When a religion suffers from spiritual senile decay, the people become too dependent upon half-frozen forms and a far-off Deity through the offices of an unillumined priesthood. The backs of the latter become loaded with theological lumber, and the backs of the former with antiquated futilities. That which should have been as a divine voice to the living, grows dreary and dull, unable to meet actual needs and constantly harking back to the dead past. Can we blame young men who hesitate to entrust their spiritual destiny to those who utter dreary platitudes about divinity, but show so little of it themselves ? Priests whose dogmas are as iron-clad and as intolerant as they can make them ; preachers who are more concerned about pew-rents than about spiritualizing their own selves ; clergymen who are prisoners of disproved doctrines which belong to their cloth ; gaitered bishops who make the mistake of imagining that a religious organization must be propped up by the State, backed by its power and fed by its finances, instead of the Church being inspired enough and vital enough to back up the State with its spiritual energy; clerics who pour out insufferable cant and sanctified tomfoolery, their hollow words re-echoed back by the walls of half-empty churches; persecutors who have failed to grasp the first letter of the alphabet of true religion, thus meriting Montesquieu's sagely cynical sentence wherein he begged them "if they could not behave as Christians, to behave at least as men!"—all these sightless servitors of an unreal God should not deplore the shortcomings of our generation but attend to their own.

♣

Four and a half centuries ago a man arose from his highest spiritual trance and taught India the Truth. "There is no Hindu and no Mussalman." And he told the Brahmins that "a real priest is he who knows God." Then he, Guru Nanak, born among the Hindus, went to Muhammedan Mecca and there said to Sheikh Farid: "Allah is ever the subject of my efforts, O Farid. Allah is ever my object."

♣

It is better to approach this tortuous subject in a direct manner. No true church of God would urge its followers to hatred of their fellows, and one that does so is rather an institution of the devil, all the mummery of its claims and rites notwithstanding. No organization dare hiss hate at all heretics through its broken teeth and expect us to believe that it does so in the name of Him who said : " On earth, peace, and goodwill to all men." Perhaps the sharpest nail in the side of gentle Jesus was struck, not in his own days, but at a later time, when the doctrines of salvation were preached with the aid of the torture-rack, the burning faggots and the executioner's block. It is to the merit of a "heathen" religion like Buddhism that it has never needed and never sought to propagate the idea of a spiritual life by such horrors ; that it has not had to commend its rational truths by means of the axe or to suppress the irrepressible reason of man by other delicate means. Pseudo-religions alone have attempted to spread their doctrines, which could not be forced into man's heads through intelligence, by torturing them into men's bodies on the rack. I thank my lucky star that I do not live in times when the hierarchs of Church and State deemed it necessary to give such misguided men as myself a few twinges of the thumbscrew every now and again, if they did not do worse and finish the job at the stake. And even if our epoch does not burn us, but merely sneers at us, we can endure a sneer better than we can endure a fire!

♣

It never occurs to most priests and most clergymen that the mystic may be much more engaged on God's work than they are—even though he be creedless, churchless and sermonless.

♣

The truth is that we ought to distrust and discard any doctrine that claims to be of God, yet dares to exclude any of God's children from its range or from the consolations of its creed. We ought to be rightly suspicious of men who talk glibly of God, but who behave like the devil, however sincere their motive. It may seem startling to the popular mind to be told that if it does not want a blank atheism, it need not therefore have a doubtful fanaticism, but it is true. The faithful of every religion try to corral God for themselves alone; the foolish of every creed think He narrows down His wide love to their particular flock. But His children must necessarily be found among Christians, Jews, Muslims, Hindus, Confucians and Atheists, among those who belong to some creed or to none, among every caste and counting: for He is the Supreme Father of all without exception, else He could not be God.

♣

The Adima and Heva of the Hindu Bible—*The Vedas*—is re-echoed again by the Adam and Eve of the Hebrew Bible. The wise see a common source for both references; the prejudiced see but a borrowing and a plagiarism; the intolerant perceive only blind imposture and wilful forgery. The real history of early man may be revealed to the creedless, but remains blank to the biased. The naked truth is too naïve for them; it must be dressed up in its coloured clothes of myth and fable. Thus the first race of men is narrowed down to the first fabled man.

♣

Dull formal piety and mute unthinking acceptance do not chime in with the mental needs of to-day. The old days when the guardians of a dogmatic religion inevitably became, as history instructs us, the gaolers of men's minds and attempted to stem the upward flow of human thought, are gone. The faith which is to guide the modern world, wheresoever it arises and whosoever is its inspirer, will have to bear an intellectual face. The rise of an age of reason is unfortunately but inexorably putting an end to religious services that lack the spirit of true religion, and to priestly figures who represent no nobler god than their own little selves. Blindly held creeds, comfortable places in which to sleep though they were, do not satisfy the modern temperament. We want to know the how and why and wherefore of things, including religion. Like bent and withered old women, twentieth-century religious organizations still go on mumbling the old stupidities of that irrational version of the Hebrew Scriptures which, even more than one thousand years ago, St. Augustine said was too childish to be considered. Because a group of Israelites got together at least ten centuries after Moses and codified their scattered traditions into a set of books, and because a second group of Christians did the same thing three or four hundred years after Christ, millions of men are no longer to think, to use the intelligence with which God has endowed them, but are to accept these dead men's opinions for all time as from God delivered. But the brilliant victories of Voltaire, who swayed the society of his time by the syllogisms of his devastating logic, began to clear the air of stale odours of superstition, and the decades since his death have carried on the process. To be asked to believe in dusty dogmas merely because they are so old, thus bringing faith into collision with reason, is to stultify true progress. The crude conception of ignorant priests and unthinking followers that the world began only a few thousand years ago, that the wonderful and intricate bodies of mankind were developed in a few minutes by the hand of God, and that the divine soul was then added to these bodies as a sort of afterthought—these stupidities are necessarily vanishing into thin air beneath the blows delivered by geological, biological and psychological science.

♣

We need not lose our common sense in order to keep our conscience.

♣

We live in the most sceptical age of all history. We breathe in an atmosphere of ardent debate and acrimonious distrust. Faith is to many the most foolish word in the twentieth-century dictionary. The reason for all that is plain. The gullible stupidity of our forefathers has created the scepticism of to-day. Those who are willing to accept the venerable nonsense which was mixed with the truth that once held prescriptive sway over the religiously minded, have diminished into a minority. Science and history have boldly and unsparingly scrutinized the traditional records of religion, and has left them in the form of tattered scraps. Scriptures packed with picturesque fables and impossible figures, with genuine revelations adulterated by queer superstitions, cannot serve the educated twentieth century, unless they are edited and revised. And who is there among us competent to do that? Truth must now be taught in clear language and with scientific exactitude, or it will hardly serve at all. Reason, rising to the ascendant in man's horoscope, demands that a presentation of Truth shall therefore be rational. If it cannot be convinced, it will not permit itself to be cajoled.

♣

Though the whole world is denied him, yet even the blindest man may see God.

♣

The new faith of our time will no longer require its advocates to believe and preach a primitive mixture of nonsense and wisdom, of ignorance and truth, but to be bound by no doctrine, to take the whole range of spiritual truth for their own, and to preach only that which their conscience and reason can keep together in perfect concord. It will herald a coming co-ordination between religion, science and philosophy. Religion must become rational; rationalism must become religious. Such is the solution which the modern age will work out. If twentieth-century people are to receive any help from ancient doctrines, they may welcome that gladly, but only if they are permitted to give the welcome with unfettered hands; they should not be required to tie themselves to the corpses of outworn dogmas. And even the rules of life will be treated in the same manner. For ancient rules of living, which were formulated in holy writs at a time when their framers could not have anticipated present-day conditions, are not necessarily binding upon us of this epoch. The Divine Wisdom which, through some prophet, gave birth to those outworn rules, can now give birth to new ones also. It is not so helpless that, having once spoken, it has been struck dumb for all time thereafter. And we are the creatures of the age in which we live. We are born to express the mind and heart of the twentieth century, and not of the third. Therefore a religion which was formed to appeal to the men of the third century may possibly leave us cold. A formal system, if it is to be propagated to-day, must be freshly born. Our future is with the divine Overself, not with those ancient scriptures covered with dust. For religion is but a manifestation of Truth. Religion is merely a bucketful of water given to a particular people; the well itself is the Truth. The well is not exhausted because two or three bucketfuls have been drawn up and shared out. Let us dip down once again and bring up a crystalline draught fit to be drunk by our own day and age. But although the technique of the spiritual life must change to suit our changed epoch, let us remember that its bedrock is eternal—the surrender of the personal self to the divine Overself.

♣

Love is the most powerful force in the universe. That is why the Supreme Being must ultimately conquer the world. For He loves His creatures so much that they will all yield themselves completely to Him one day.

♣

The modern world cannot digest the cruel and crude doctrine of eternal damnation; will it be able to digest the rational and sweeter doctrine of eternal salvation? All are to be saved and brought to the Highest, because all contain the God-atom in their hearts.

CHAPTER VIII

INTELLECT

Although we may foresee the necessity of religion taking an intellectual incarnation if it is to appeal to present-day needs, this is not to say that we are therefore to continue with the present exaggerated worship of intellect. The latter, too, has its painful limitations and suffers from the same blindness in refusing to see those limitations. In fact, the reverence for intellect becomes farcical when pushed to extremes : If Christ came to-day He would be expected to bear the M.A. and B.Litt.

♣

The Sages do not need to buttress Truth with the vicious circle of argument.

♣

The intellectual wealth of the whole world is now ours, but we are barely wiser. We still wonder why the earth was made and what is the meaning of life. We would still like to learn the art of self-control and the way to undisturbed happiness. We are still disturbed by some unexpected flash of interrogative thought which moves across our minds and asks why a good God can permit evil and suffering. We would still like to learn the secret of death and to be able to answer the question: "Is the beauty of woman to be but the prey of the worm?" Life, which stretches all the way from the illusory to the illimitable, remains ever the most tantalizing of problems.

When the modern chemist discovered that the atom was not the last word on the material side of things, and that the so-called physical universe pales away into an unseen and practically unknown Force, every profound thinker must have known that the death-blow had been given to the gospel of gross materialism.

The materialistic intellectual insists on taking one position: He insists on standing on his head and then studying the universe as he sees it. Because he can see only the dark earth, he hastens to the conclusion that this is the all-Existent.

If only he would trouble to reverse himself, he might then perceive the sky as well as the earth, and thus gain a truer perspective. This is a far-fetched picture, I know, but it conveys my plaint of his one-sidedness. He uses the faculty of observation and the faculty of reason, applies both to a study of the world, but will not apply them to a study of himself. Oh yes, he is willing to study the outer fringe of self, the passions and thoughts which throb through his personality, but he is totally unwilling to penetrate deeper and find out WHO is behind that personality.

♣

Learning is good as a step upon the road to realization of the Overself, but it is bad as a grave in which to bury our heads and hearts.

♣

Logic is a remarkably useful instrument. We can perform many useful and necessary operations of a commercial, domestic, practical or professional nature with its aid. Nevertheless both history and experience tell us that logic is often used to substantiate a lie. As a matter of fact the superficial find logic a useful means of proving one's self right, however wrong. Thus they impose upon people who accept anything, however fallacious, provided it is presented to them disguised with the externals of logical proof. Logic is an admirable servant to a wise employer but verily it is a bad master. In the service of a fool it becomes more unreliable as it becomes more lucid. We cannot stop fools from buckling on their logic as proof, while they, like the knightly Don Quixote, cannot stop mistaking basins for helmets. And the ceremonials of logic can be made to serve, in expert hands, two contending doctrines with equal facility. So, although we need not throw this instrument away, we must sometimes watch its use warily. Materialism, for instance, depends on such kind of logic for its support. The materialists have built up a great superstructure of able reasoning ; the exactness of their thinking and the accuracy of their logic cannot but command our respect. Yet through all the years when their system was being erected it never occurred to them to look to the quality of their foundations. It has never occurred to them that their data might be one-sided and their premises incomplete. Their keen intellects have skilfully built up brick upon brick of the consequences resulting from their doctrines, yet they have been unable to perceive that the fundamental postulates of those doctrines are true only in part. This is not to deny that their conclusions may be quite correct from the standpoint they have adopted, but only to say that to " stand upon one's head " does not provide the best observations upon which one's logic is to work. To stand upon one's SELF —that which views the world—first, and then to reverse, is a complete and correct procedure.

♣

Intellectual judgments will always carry the dogs of doubt and debate fastened to their tails, if not of denial. Direct spiritual perception is alone free and alone conveys complete certitude. By that I do not mean theological theorizing. I refer to something within man which *knows*. " God does not reason. Why should you reason if you know ? " demanded a Hindu Sage. The abrupt flash of intuition is the Sage's spiritual reward, replacing in him the long and laborious workings of ratiocination.

♣

Though our world has said farewell to blind spiritual faith, it need not say farewell to spiritual investigation.

♣

Yet whoever says that spiritual truth must

contradict logic is talking twaddle. The former is big enough and broad enough to take a hundred logics in its stride and absorb them all. Every canon of the divine wisdom fits in with the canons of faultless logic. I have wandered through the wide domain of Professor Jevons' amiable science, travelled from premise to conclusion, and struggled with the intricacies of the syllogism, but never once have I found it necessary to pitch my mysticism overboard. If a short-sighted intellectual tells me that higher truth must necessarily be false because it is mystical and therefore cannot be logical, I must perforce turn round and tell him to go and get a deeper experience of life and not limit himself to the narrow round of book, bread and bank. If he has only applied his logic to the outer world and thinks it cannot be applied successfully to any expression of spiritual truth, that is not the fault of such truth but his own. Let him arise out of his little corner of life and go through the search and suffering every true mystic has to endure, and then, mayhap, he will return a silent man, abashed at his former foolishness and conscious of the perfect, irrefutable logic which pervades every nook and cranny of our universe.

♣

The machine-like motion of the ratiocinating

faculty has killed many truths that were just being cradled by semi-intuitive men.

♣

Emotion is a more powerful driving force than intellect: we usually try to find reasons for our feelings; it is seldom the other way about.

♣

We must not imagine that we acquire knowledge each time we acquire a book. There are ponderous tomes which look so wise with their grave-faced bindings, and which appear so learned with their multitude of quotations, that we fall into delusion about their real quality: sometimes the amount of real intelligence they contain is in inverse proportion to their size. They may be a help to talk, but not to Truth. Sterile intellectuals who sit and brood endlessly over the addled eggs of theoretical speculation add nothing to our store of true knowledge. Why should we listen with such awe to the last pronouncements of the professors? One reads a hundred pages of their profound web-spinning, and one begins to feel like that hapless yokel on the London Inner Circle subway train who arrived nowhere! One turns to a single sentence of the Indian Upanishads five lines long and perhaps five thousand years old, and one finds both intellectual meat and drink, and one is less bored withal. The latest production of the University is not necessarily the last word of the Universe! An academic will think nothing of peering into his mental-wardrobe for an Opinion or of taking out some dusty *suit* of a Theory, and offering it to foolish clients with the brazen remark that it is a perfect fit for Truth, when, in fact, it is so tight at the shoulders and so baggy at the knees that it would be better wear for a scarecrow.

The intellectual argues, but the Sage announces.

Science is indubitably of genuine interest and evident worth to the world, but super-science is no less interesting and infinitely more valuable. But just as it is the intellectual faculty which is the mainspring of scientific culture, so is it the intuitive faculty which is the mainspring of super-science. Yet our proud intellectuals often do not hesitate to declare, because they are unable to pack the Infinite and Absolute into the small box of bone which holds their brain, that there is no Infinite and Absolute. Such is their temerity. One can appreciate the remarkable work done by experimental and applied science, without admiring the disastrous results which a neglect of spiritual super-science has brought upon us. The blank oblivion of the basic facts behind human existence which covers so many minds to-day is part of the dire punishment.

♣

Despite the learned and lengthy volumes of our professors, we still know little of the baffling mystery of the mind. But the Sage, having plumbed its depths, will explain its true nature in a few words.

♣

The new phyeicists have explained away Matter, but our Intellects can follow them only theoretically. There is, however, an intuitive faculty in man which, though generally dormant, can follow them in a very real way. Our consciousness of the solid world depends upon the senses, which in their turn are our means of apprehending Matter. If we could withdraw consciousness from the senses for a time, in a state of full awareness, we would then necessarily withdraw it from Matter. And what would we find ? A vacuum ? We would find the spiritual world of being, so much spoken of by the great seers and sages of all times. To effect that withdrawal, we need to suspend temporarily the action of intellect and allow the ignored intuitive faculty to come into sway. But how many of us, inordinately proud of intellect and its achievements as we are, would be willing to do that ? Yet unless we do that we shall never fulfil the higher purpose of our birth, never find the true kingdom of heaven.

♣

We moderns have been so busy studying the world without that we have largely forgotten to study the world within.

♣

It would even be better, were it necessary, which it is not, to throw all our past learning into a bonfire and forget it, than to let it stand constantly in the way of our attainment of this higher purpose. The call of man's spiritual self is supremely more important than the call of his mental machine. The first is divine and will, when answered and obeyed, bestow lasting happiness ; the second is mechanical and can give but transient satisfaction.

♣

I am frankly afraid of some of our highbrow intellectuals. I try never to discuss a thing with them, but maintain a Pythagorean silence before their babble of torrential speech. For they have a way of using words that are wiser than their thoughts ; their thoughts may be as shallow as a summer's ditch, but the words in which they are wrapped are deep enough and ponderous enough to make even those who use them stand in awe at their own wisdom. If philosophy is nowadays too often relegated to the attic, as having no bearing upon the practical affairs of life, then philosophers themselves are to blame. The basis of their mental edifice should be here, among the facts of mundane existence, and not only among the theoretical notions which fill the shelves of libraries. Nor is the possession of a little literary facility any proof of truth : often it is nothing but a mere outlet for the writers. The unspiritual intellectual condemns me because he cannot comprehend me. I condemn him because I can comprehend him. The sceptic who proposes to examine the mystic, and comes along with an attitude of mind that regards the latter as a fool or knave, closes the very doors he thinks he is going to open. He may bear the serious face of study and yet be far away from true knowledge, being the mere dupe of opinion and the shuttlecock of other minds.

♣

But my final plaint against the over-intellectual

is that he would reject an inspired writing because it lacks syllogistic strength : he is thus comparable to those who would reject a diamond because it is in the crude, unpolished state. Logic is his Deity. There is hardly a truth which can stand the acid of well-directed logic, and a clever critic could destroy any man's veridical vision. Archbishop Whately proved with pleasant irony, by publishing *Historic Doubts Relative to Napoleon*, that there is no fact which cannot be disbelieved on good logical grounds. The truth is that the over-intellectual makes his own mental and spiritual groove and spends the rest of his life running up and down it. With the result that he aptly illustrates the thought that prompted the poet Byron to write :

> " How little do we know that which we are !
> How less what we may be ! "

Those who are wedded to a philosophy of words, or who have been rendered haughty by the scraps of knowledge they have picked up out of the infinite storehouse, need to be questioned after the searching method of Socrates before they can be put into the right attitude to learn.

CHAPTER IX

MUSIC, MASK AND PEN

Jazz, once the music of the jungle, barbaric, unrefined, is now the music of this age. We live in a jazz-minded world, where everything that is noisy, everything that is blatant, is sure of a hearing. Beauty, dignity, refinement and quietness tend to be forgotten, and we who care for them must await their return in loneliness. One can scarcely call jazz a form of music, although well-meaning ones try to convince us that it is the latest and therefore the highest evolution of music. It is a rhythm of the moment, shaking the debris of past centuries out of our bodies and hearts, but it is an unpleasant rhythm. It is a fit parallel to our modern life, which is a light laugh on the surface, but a bitter cry underneath. The misery and materialism of our saxophonic world is aptly synchronized with the fact that the raucous soul-destroying jazz-drum is more popular than the sweet and soft violin. We revel in jazz whilst we reel to we know not what.

We carp at elevation of mind and nobility of spirit, but dance away ecstatically when we get into the mud of plantation jazz, for there we find a harmonious home. We wallow in its vulgarity simply because we like it. The jazz and dancing with which we surround ourselves are so much make-believe, so much compensation for the spiritual failure of our lives. Dancing to a strident jazz tune, conventionally correct though it be, lets the pantherine animal of loose character creep underneath our smooth skins. The morals of the world are as chaotic as the music it prefers. Music, which can rise to the heights of being a welcome whisper from God to man, sinks to the level of being a salacious noise. Music, which can be a divine voice reminding us of our ancestral spiritual home, now savagely tries to stampede us back to the barbarian. Music, which could tell of ideal love between man and woman, drags that love into stupid slush. I much prefer to listen to the chirruping swallows at sunrise than to a noisy jazz band at sunset, or to turn from the noisy world and listen to the subtle strains that remind one of the spirits' ancestral home? Who can hear the immortal music of Beethoven's *Minuet in G*, for instance, without feeling some yearning for a life more beautiful, an existence more spiritual?

Pleasure is our easy substitute for Happiness.

♣

Stage and cinema continue to specialize in their portrayal of one facet of life, and that a dubious one. They delight in offering us the adventures of those amorous and amiable gentlemen who wander without compass but with roving eyes, seeking licentious adventure. They treat such minor things as husbands as almost negligible in the scale of utilities. It would appear, if we are to follow their sophisticated guidance, that women enter the state of matrimony in order to possess the praised pleasure of finding lovers outside matrimony; that they look for loyalty in every man except their own husbands; that they live to delight every husband but their own; and that they form easy prey for the gay wife-hunters of our time. If I were to believe the drama, modern wives are but light-footed Venuses in constant transit from their husbands' arms to those of some nocturnal lover; and modern men are twentieth-century Don Juans, elegant and gilded beings with nothing better to do than to go out seeking whom they may seduce, their sugared words masked in the name of love.

♣

Such muddy morals may represent the decadence of our epoch or they may not, but they offer a form of suggestion whose power is under-estimated or ignored. It is very entertaining to take these glances at the passions of the night through the screen or stage, but it is unlikely to help our own morals if we make a habit of it. Suggestion is a force ; thought heaped on thought tends with time to turn its begetter into dark alleys that may surprise him. Our unbridled age would be none the worse for a few anti-aphrodisiacs through the same medium. The creeping paralysis of the best in man which has been going on around us receives far too much support from playwrights and scenario writers. They sweep up the dark corners of crime and sex, and empty the dustpan for the benefit of their audiences. For life is a large whirlpool and the scum rises quicker to the surface. These writers mistake this scum for the real water. Sex and crime constitute the pabulum for their efforts. An intelligent observer, arriving here from another planet, would therefore conclude that sex and crime occupied the greater part of our time. The tragedies of crime and lust which are enacted on the boards and the screen may form delectable diversions to us ; really they are sinister attractions offering unconscious suggestions. A man's business is not to submit himself to influences which degrade, but to elevate his thoughts and ennoble his emotions.

♣

The youthful screen-struck flapper sighs and yearns for her cave-man, her adored Sheikh. When she gets him she finds he is nothing but a bully. Thus another cinema-born romance is rudely broken. And once the clown was enough to amuse the mob ; now nothing short of the screen-criminal will suffice.

♣

Sensuality is rewarded, while spirituality is snubbed. The sensual cinema star, who plays up the frivolous emotions of flappers and weak-willed trouser-wearers, may hope to become a dollar millionaire ; the selfless sage, who bestows his years and energy in the sublime and noble search for Truth on his own and mankind's behalf, may hope to become a pauper.

♣

The masses, who anciently worshipped God and revered His prophets, now worship in cinema-temples and revere screen-stars. Sex and crime to-day get all the glory and all the romance. Rightly handled, with inspired men at the helm and inspired stories on the screen, the cinema might help educate our masses into the astonishing discovery of their spiritual selves, the most wonderful of all romances. Instead, it is helping them into spiritual heedlessness.

♣

Man's cleverness has contorted the face of vice into the visage of virtue. Adultery, which was once regarded as a regrettable sin, is now regarded as a commendable part of every married couple's experience, if we are to heed the hints provided by our Gallicized stage.

♣

Song, stage and cinema offer remarkably effective mediums to serve the constructive causes in life; great art of any kind can inspire man to true satisfaction and nobler thought. Instead, we let the masses derive a spurious satisfaction from spurious enjoyments.

♣

If one were to judge by the outstanding successes on the stage, the libertine, the gangster and the crook are the heroes of the mob, whether the latter are Bowery born or Mayfair bred. We watch with avidity the exploits of a man of loose morals and hail eagerly the adventures of a criminal whose entry into our lives would hardly be permitted.

Those books are common to-day which express in noble language the mean thoughts of petty persons. We prefer litter to literature. How poor does our modern output seem because it lacks the divine quality which animated many of the ancient writers, who took their start on the reality of the gods and who drew their inspiration from the sacred well of the soul. The writers of antiquity were not wholly fools. There are plenty of living truths written down in the so-called dead languages. There is more sound sense in a single volume of Epictetus' talks as recorded in the Greek tongue than in fifty volumes by many a noted author of to-day. There is better guidance and no less enthralling interest in the stories of a neglected ancient work like *The Yoga Vasishta*, as written down by the bard Valmiki in Sanskrit, than in shelves full of belauded modern books. To descend from the fine inspirations of such ancients in order to listen to the mental mutterings of our modern psychological novelists is sometimes like stepping into a home for morbid neurasthenics or entering a divorce court and listening to salacious testimony, or squeezing into a crowded night club full of cocktail-tipplers, or drinking a concoction of criminal episodes under the impression that it is a good thing for one's health.

♣

Our age will readily read the audacious egotists, but turns a bored head away when an illumined sage ventures to write quietly about the truths which lie at the foundations of life. We may admit that the brilliant twaddle of many of our moderns is better than the dull twaddle of the last century, but is it more important than twaddle ?

♣

To read is to borrow another man's thoughts.

♣

Our greatest illusion is disillusion. We imagine that we are disillusioned with life, when the truth is that we have not even begun to live. Scrawlers and scribblers pepper their novels with sighing soliloquies or fill the air with thwarted desires ; knowing next to nothing about spiritual life—which is the secret import of our existence—they are therefore deputed to portray man's social possibilities. We place puerile effusions upon our shelves, but have little room for volumes of eternal value. When one reads a book, one travels with the soul of another man. We ought, therefore, to take no less care with the company of printed pages that we peruse than with the company of men and women among whom we mingle.

♣

People prefer chloroform ; tell them what they already know or what they have already thought a hundred times, and they will be pleased with your writings. Give them worn-to-a-thread stories and they will recommend your book to their friends. Offer them something fit for Babitts, not for thinking men, and they will hail your work. Serve up ideas which are nothing but dusty platitudes, write much but succeed in saying little, or have nothing to say but many words in which to say it, use a pen which suffers from pronounced senility, offer a wordy and windy exposition of your theme, and you may hope to become a leviathan of modern literature.

♣

The few write for posterity, the many for prosperity !

♣

In all sincere writing one never consciously

seeks to be clever, never tries to arouse those brilliant powers of wit and expression which move the pens of gifted minds. That which comes out of the tip of one's nib must flow of its own accord or not at all. Yet when I write down what seems to me plain and obvious truth, I am amazed to hear carping critics exclaim: "He is trying to be clever!"

♣

The pointed sallies of the cynic may be entertaining and diverting, but unless they are complemented by the inspiring intuitions of the prophet they do not contribute to that constructive effort on its behalf of which the whole world is in need. Criticism should be constructive; it should not degenerate into mere vituperation; it should not replace argument by acrimonious railing, either. Nor, in one's zest to propagate a single truth, is it necessary to trample down all other truths, or become like those noisy authors who appear to write through a megaphone.

♣

Our clever moderns do not find it tedious to read refined trash, but they are exceedingly bored when presented with a book which gives voice to the immortal self.

♣

Those who regard our "thrillers" and books written around criminal adventurous episodes as mysterious are often mistaken; the latter are often banal and commonplace. We believe we have gone one better than our tame ancestors in producing them; we of this twentieth century pride ourselves on making life and literature more interesting. As a matter of fact there are no real mysteries in our times really worth writing about, whereas there were "the Ancient Mysteries" among most ancient nations because they had many spiritual and psychic secrets to take care of.

♣

In the old days a book generally took its place in literature; it is too often to-day no more than an extended newspaper article, a piece of journalese, supplying tit-bits of information for those who can only take their reading in the form of scrappy pieces of light knowledge, and who shut their eyes to the shining stars in the literary firmament capable of giving light to man's soul and of bringing beauty into his life. Those who possess the minds of midgets can only be expected to skim upon the surface of life. They grudge the time required by a pithy and pregnant book, which imposes a little labour in thinking upon those who would understand what they read.

♣

We like books only where they think for us. Nor do we care for those who dare to think too deeply for us; while we prefer the author who mistakes molecular disturbances in his brain for creative thoughts.

♣

"The pen is mightier than the sword." It is not for me, peaceable citizen that I am, to dispute that idealistic statement. Yet, in times of war even the hand-grenade may prove more paramount than the paragraph, while the pen may be a little weaker than a whizz-bang.

♣

The flowers of literature can bloom only for those who appreciate the charm of style, the dignity of real learning and the inspiration of profound thought. Word merchants, who set out to tickle the taste of the moment, that is to say, to satisfy the vulgar and profane, may dispense with these last-named. But, for their soul's sakes they might find better employment following the plough rather than plying the pen. From the quiet transcendental literature of bygone ages down to the saxophonic literature of the modern age is a long step, for it is a step out of eternal values into meretricious materialism. The ancient authors built better sky-scrapers than ever America did, ones which are certain to endure whilst intelligence and good feeling remain among us, but the giant garish towers of many moderns shall have their day.

♣

Some are born writers : others take correspondence courses !

♣

The Fable is a neglected literary form which the ancients highly valued and whose importance they well understood. The world has deserted this pithy condensed form for the more voluminous novels and the thick book of essays, but I think it will recognize its error one day. There is room in literature for all three. For the Fabulist conveys worth-while wisdom, but not its heaviness, and moralizes without dullness. He instructs the erring and admonishes the wicked, but does it all without boring them.

♣

The Press need not lose its manners in order to carry out its duty of supplying information ; it need not turn a man's private existence into a public secret against his will, nor make excessive capital out of the shame, tragedy and misfortune of our lives. A clean, sane Press would help to produce clean, sane citizens. Those who sensationalize or exaggerate the simplest piece of news, who sacrifice truth and decency for the sake of stunt-making, who gloat over frailties and sensualities, do not realize their responsibility. The printed page has, to a large extent, become the modern pulpit. What sort of sermons do our modern newspapers preach ?

♣

If the proprietors of newspapers spent half their money and a quarter of their staff's energy on obtaining news and comment of a higher kind, they might let their earthly frames go, at the appointed hour, knowing that a load of sins had been atoned for. Our journals cannot devote enough space to the most important matters because they devote so much to trivial ones, and to disgusting crimes, scandals and sensations. There is no right proportion in these things. The pathetic pursuit of mere speed is well exemplified in daily journalism and poisons our existence with futile excitements. Every event is given a brief, hasty life as it is whirled through a two or three days' career in print, and then forgotten by a public too weak to resist the next sensation forced upon its enfeebled mind. A passion of the night, as displayed in some scandal, stirs a million hearts who read about it in print, but a vital topic upon which mankind's true happiness depends is given a line or ignored through the fear that the mis-educated reading public will be left cold with an Arctic frigidity.

♣

A journalist is a man who can formulate, at five minutes' notice, a fixed opinion upon any subject under the sun—including those which have left the great philosophers in baffled doubt and perplexed despair for centuries.

♣

Enterprising editors take care to keep boredom out of their papers by filling their pages with things which are merely incidental to life or abnormal to it. Instead of offering us so many reports of dissolved marriages, they might try to report the happiness of the undissolved ones, and thus perform a much-needed constructive service to present-day humanity. Instead of revealing the grim details of how death took the last breath from a murdered man, they might try to reveal the details of how true happiness came to a living one. Instead of indulging in orgies of sensational details about unpleasant matters, let them—if they must refer to such things—merely announce the fact and be done with it. Instead of making the jockey who wins a fifteen-minute race into a public hero, they might endeavour to find a real hero of the inner life. Instead of fostering national and international hatreds, they might see what they could do to foster goodwill in the same quarters.

It might be thought that a newspaper that printed only worth-while news instead of stupidities, crimes and stunts, could have no place in the modern world, but I do not agree. A newspaper built on a basis of spirituality in action, which would carry Truth to the masses and be unafraid to work for spiritual ideals, which would apply spiritual principles in its handling of material affairs, which would link conscience to its courage and inspiration to its opinion, might surprise the world by its success. It could be something more than a mere journalistic Argosy; it could be a prophetic voice crying in the wilderness of modern materialism, a finger pointing towards the future of mankind in this country, and if it did its work well it need not fail. Its reporters could search for news of every event that could bring satisfaction to the minds of decent people, every movement that was working to better the common good, every person who is a benefactor to mankind; and they could find printable stories of the Good, the True and the Beautiful. Writers who were not mere mercenaries, who possessed a few sparks of idealism, who realized that they had a duty in this age, could be found and would be glad to serve such a journal. What grander task could they find, anyhow, than contributing their hands towards the spiritual revival of their race, and the elevation of the collective society of their country. That is true patriotism, not the mean thing which hates other people in the name of its own. The first function of a newspaper was to be a clear mirror of life; to-day it has become a powerful maker of life.

♣

We hear much of the need of abandoning ideals

if the creative artist is to produce something more than mere bread. Carlyle once defined genius as the capacity for taking infinite pains. It is likely that many geniuses do not agree with him, and that they would say: Genius is the capacity for taking infinitesimal pay! For the inspired artist, whether of pen or brush or mallet, reaches an agonising moment when he has to choose between the chasm of joining the general scramble for making more money and the abyss of eking out a penurious livelihood. If, as mostly happens, the better-paid work wins and his fervour fades away with defeat, his rebellion changing into resignation, we may yet recognize the true nature of his struggle and respect the sublime source which induced him to make it.

♣

There are worse fates for the sincere writer than to become his only reader!

CHAPTER X

SOLITUDE AND LEISURE

We cannot escape from the essential loneliness of our individual nature. We may attempt to cover it up by social duties, work, personal ties and conventional thinking, but in the momentous crises of life or at the deepest points of our direst agonies, we discover that we are unutterably alone, that we have bartered the soul's strength for an estate of thorns and briars. Nature has imposed this condition upon us, but society conspires to hide it from us for long stretches of time. In reality we are isolated beings. We suffer because we refuse to recognize that fact and because we try to outwit that condition which Nature has bestowed upon us. But the moment we admit and recognize it we receive added strength and renewed peace. " The strongest man is he who stands most alone," announced the Scandinavian dramatist, Ibsen, in a phrase that flits frequently across my mind. This sentence suggests a train of profound truths. Not that it is necessary to become a world-shunning recluse in order to stand alone. There is a spiritual solitude, a virile independence, which a man can carry with him into the busy places of the world, and which is as much the real thing as whatever he may attain by escaping from the whirlpool into a secluded retreat. There is a profound reason for this inner loneliness of man: the attainment of the Kingdom of Heaven—which is the secret goal of living—demands retirement from any dependence on our fellows in order that we may depend on none but the Higher Power men name God. And did not Jesus tell us that the Kingdom was within us? Such retirement necessarily requires our constant turning towards the inner self, and therefore an acceptance of solitude as a thing no less desirable than society.

♣

It is a hard thing to mind your own business, your higher business—but it is worth while. Attend to your own self, your Overself, and then the cares and burdens of existence will quietly withdraw under its benign influence. Jesus put this truth into parable, but our clever theologians have missed the meaning.

♣

What applies to the genius applies equally to

other men, albeit in a lesser degree. If genius would be true to itself it must estrange itself from the world and nourish its inner life in solitary thought. Where else can it find the creative wonders that it shall give forth to the world except in its own originality? For the sight it gains in solitude is true vision. It is no less true that the average man must also find himself in solitude and spend himself in society. When he turns his back on his fellows and walks through the dark corridor of loneliness, he can arrive at himself. But few are ready to receive this thought, and the apostle of solitude must waste his voice crying in the wilderness. We have erected society as an idol, worshipping on bended knees before its smug and stupid face, and thus have come to the forgetfulness of worshipping the divinity who lies hid within our own selves. The best men are not gregarious; they are strong enough to be true to themselves. But the others—and they are in the majority—huddle together in houses, join clubs and societies, gather and foregather. Solitude is strength; to depend on the presence of the crowd is weakness. The man who needs a mob to nerve him is much more alone than he imagines. The gregarious instinct enslaves us and enfeebles us, when we must be running every hour to see our fellows in order to assure ourselves of their existence and support. It is better to distrust the quick *camaraderie* of shallow men and to move a trifle warily among them, knowing that the secret spiritual life has temporarily moated us apart from them.

The Founder of the Jesuit Order knew the value of solitude. "The more our soul finds itself alone and in seclusion," he instructed his followers, "the fitter she renders herself to approach and attain her Creator and Lord, and the nearer she draws in this manner to Him the more she prepares herself to receive graces and gifts from His Divine and Sovereign Goodness." Solitude seems a somewhat gloomy road to the house of spiritual wisdom, and in truth we may find it so for some years. But when the aspiring soul retraces its steps and mixes overmuch with company, it tires and hurries back to its lonely vigils, there to regain its central integrity. The truth is that for most men who tread the advancing way a day dawns when they have to choose between the solitary life of the Overself and the gregarious existence of the flesh. The bright sun they follow lures them into a lone path. And although we think that we walk the grey world alone, if we are sincere it is not so. Ministering spirits come to soothe us, friendly thoughts arrive to companion us, strange, unseen hands come forth out of the darkness to help us, angelic figures may guide us, and if we rest awhile we may catch half-heard voices breaking through the once-dreaded silence and whispering comfort and consolation.

♣

A wise solitude thus fosters the soul's growth, keeps the mind clear of petty thoughts and matures the fine quality of mental independence. Go your way alone and you walk a path that shall indeed arrive somewhere. For solitude is not loneliness, boredom, or sadness. To be lonely is to be amongst those that do not understand. But in solitude you can people your place with thoughts, if you wish, whilst you always have yourself, your Overself, for company. "Let me alone," cried the lobster in Kingsley's *The Water Babies*, "I want to think!" thus showing that it is a natural instinct to seek for solitude when the need of meditation is felt. "I have learnt more," said Sir Thomas Palmer, that talented friend of Cranmer, as he prepared to lay his head before the executioner's axe, "in a dark corner of the Tower than in travelling around Europe." While somewhere in the Bible the phrase runs: "And he went up into the mountain to pray, himself, alone."

♣

There are sages in the East who find a better friendship in their own minds than in society. We sneer at the men who flee from crowded cities and prefer to please themselves in lonely places. We talk foolishly of their cowardice. But to accept the gregarious comfort of the crowd may be an easier act than to go into retirement and face one's own self. Who knows but that solitude, which might easily drive superficial men to madness, may restore others to true sanity? We are frightened at the mere suggestion of retreating from the crowd and live as though safety were in stupid numbers alone. The sage who sits in sublime harmony with the best thoughts and noblest ideals, though he live in a forest, is not lonely. You might as well call the sun lonely. There he can profitably forget the world, knowing that he can now remember himself, his true self, his Overself. Bacon was not unduly harsh when he indicted society in that mordant sentence: "A crowd is not company, faces are but a gallery of pictures and talk but a tinkling of cymbals where there is no love."

♣

Your self is sacred; be true to it.

♣

The sister of solitude is leisure and its cousin

is the country-side. Those who are habitants of the busy towns would do well to flee the turmoil and go now and again into some quiet wood or beside some gentle stream, not only for restorative air, but also where they can search for beauty and light and truth—unless they are dead to these things. There they can find elbow room enough, and to spare. And then, when they leave their Londons, their familiar streets filled with hurrying pedestrians and snorting motors, and enter the first country lane, they are undone. Their cleverness stops at the sight of green Nature. She speaks no word of wisdom into their ears, offers no spectacle of charm to their eyes. Life suddenly becomes an awful blank and time changes into a boring fellow.

♣

The soul may speak to us in moments of quiet thought and in times of peaceful relaxation. Nay, it is always speaking, but in the fret and fever of active existence its voice remains unheard, its face unrecognized.

♣

I would fain put the sky between me and the

large cities and find in the solitudes of the peaceful and picturesque country-side that greatness of mood which the narrow streets would deny me. I would do what the soul demands, knowing that I shall not regret it. For there is a way of life worth having, and it is best lived among the trees, on the grass and in the lush green fields, where one finds an external reproduction of the central quietness in the soul. I need no populous city to cheer me. Nature herself is the best soother and the best healer. In a winding, beech-shaded Buckinghamshire lane watching the butterflies alight on flowering bushes, or lying down beside a meandering stream and letting my eyes rest on the marsh marigolds shining in the sunlight, the pure peace carried my mind towards life's best. Every tree and every bush brought a truer voice than I could hear among most men. I think wistfully in my Asiatic exile of those crickets that chirped at twilight, a merry sound that one heard like music. A simple red sunset descending on a pleasant landscape has put me in a holier mood than a hundred sermons. A walk in the leaf-strewn woods and silent fields during autumn, a rest in a sweet-smelling hayfield under the June sun, a tryst with the dawn on a hill-crest—these places have brought secret balm and there is no loneliness there. Best of all, one could be oneself and not have to keep one's tongue in constant operation upon talk for its own sake.

I have found the Thames every whit as holy as the Ganges. With this muddy stream I have lived in high company: Nature was my familiar and her beauty my exemplar. Wandering along its grassy banks on a sunny afternoon, after Old Sol had temped me to abandon work for a day, strolling beside the quieter reaches on the side away from Richmond and sitting down at a sequestered spot; then letting my mind slip gently back into its indescribable infinite Source—lo! within the hour I have been admitted into the serene consciousness and mysterious dimension of divinity. For me the Thames will ever flow through the assured peacefulness of Paradise and be a stream of sacred memories. Now I walk beside a wider stream and the sun which draws me thither shines in a stranger world than our own.

There is a friendliness in flowing water, an uplift in hill-sides, a stability in growing trees and a charm in coloured flowers which draws one to these things when seeking calm for the soul or inspiration for living. Even in the East I find that forests, hills, river-banks and gardens are among the places recommended by the sages to their pupils as the best places in which to practise meditation. Select some little stream upon whose surface there floats, perhaps, a few leaves and stray flowers, whither you may escape for an hour or two to dream of diviner matters. There will grow on you in such a spot a passion for solitude and an appreciation of simple beauty that your descents into society may tend to confirm. Nature will become one of your best friends and, in all the years of a long friendship, she will never once "let you down." When weariness or trouble prove too strong for you, you have but to return to her to find her arms are always ready to console you.

♣

Eagles dwell in the lonely eyries of crags and hills, but sparrows twitter plentifully in the cities.

♣

> "We have no time to stand and stare,
> No time to stand beneath the boughs,
> And stare as long as sheep or cows"

—sings the tramp poet, W. H. Davies. The true

luxury is leisure. But the leisure must be rightly used, must become an opportunity for spiritual return and not for noisy excitement, if it is to profit us truly. Quietude is the beginning of wisdom. The stars do their work, but make no noise. Power comes from and after peace. We exhaust our resources in a ceaseless centrifugal life. Wise Nature imposes forced sleep upon us, because we have not yet learnt to balance our external activity with centripetal repose. Even the hours which are given to so-called leisure vibrate with hectic stimulants and nerve tensions. Thus the human battery is short-circuited in its power. Some of us would sooner brave physical dangers than sit for an hour or two to gather a high mood. People cannot indulge their passion for activity—whether in work or pseudo-leisure—without paying the price. In the rush and roar of Western civilization it is indeed a hard task to reverse one's effort and let go of things. But we ought not to let the dust of our restless existence obscure our spiritual sight. We need to profit by our leisure and stand aside frequently from the endless procession of events which we foolishly believe contain the all of living. We need to steal a little real leisure as often as possible, when we can live for an hour quiet and content, care-free and untrammelled, raised above the servile slaveries of city life and no longer governed by the clock.

The tree of silence may produce the pears of wisdom, if we water it in solitude.

Why waste the true fragrance of life for the sake of pseudo-sensations ?

The world wants us to immerse ourselves entirely in its business and pleasures. We ought to claim a complete freedom to do nothing of the sort whenever we wish, and bid the world keep its din from our ears whenever we choose. Such leisure may bring great advantages to the harassed man of to-day. While life entraps him in the unending line of passing events, he is unable to win a true perspective. Strain, hurry and anxiety write themselves into his skin, his eyes and his mouth. He clutters up his days with robot-like activities, which affix bars and bolts to his inner progress. He is in a tremendous haste yet even while he accelerates the wheels of his own existence, nature coolly refuses to add a single unit to her own speed.

♣

We are so busy getting hold of things that we have no time to get hold of ourselves.

♣

Although I work harder than the average man, I have a great sympathy for a man who was observed to sit for hours on a log of timber in Florida. When asked about his occupation, he calmly answered that he could spare no time to work! Was he busy communing with his Overself? Who knows what rich reward he gained from his silent soliloquies?

♣

To know the Overself is to know the deep, unmoved rest which is at the centre of our being.

♣

We need to be quiet and ready for an hour if we would have the Overself speak to us; but when all our day is taken up with an endless activity, whether of work or pleasure, who is to blame but ourselves that we suffer in heart and struggle in mind ? As a first step we must free ourselves for a brief period daily from the nets of activity that are spread out for the feet of men. Grinning demons beset and pursue us to the last minute of our waking day, setting us some task to do or some pleasure to follow. Unless we drive them off for an hour, how are we to come to that deeper knowledge of ourselves which is found only in quietude of body and stillness of thought ?

♣

We spend so much of our leisure doing nothing which really matters, that there is little of it left to do the one thing that emphatically does matter.

♣

We are mad on speed. We are busy running as fast as we can—but whither ? Leisure is the lost art of the modern world. We dash into our cars and dash away at forty miles an hour in order to rush away from ourselves, our Overself, which might rise up and face us accusingly, were we to spend an hour in quiet meditation. The devastating task which Voltaire undertook is being ably continued by the motor car ! The destruction of what is false in a creed is being followed by the destruction of what is true in a creed—the unshakable fact that man must attempt to commune with his Creator, if he is to *live*. And because so few go to a church for this communion it remains for us to go to the only place where we can find it —within our own divine nature, the Overself. Yet our cars carry us away for immense distances, but only to turn leisure into further activity of one kind or another, and thus they never succeed in enabling us to arrive anywhere. Our bodies are shunted from place to place, while the soul remains inert, not having progressed a single step forward. The motor car could carry us to a leisure well worth while, if it carried us to some wood or field or stream, there to let the mind find a few elevated cloistral moments. To what end do we propose all this piling-up of horse-powers, when we exist to no other end than the divine journey towards discovery of the Overself ? The latter dwells interiorly in detached equanimity.

♣

All our travelling pursues only the path of a circle, for whever we go we succeed only in arriving at our own selves.

♣

It is true that nowadays many of us believe that

our intense activity is dictated to us by inexorable circumstances. Yet a correct attitude towards self and environment would bring a realization of the supreme importance of our private leisure, a realization which should lead us to make leisure when we do not possess the time for it. We should clearly see that even a half-hour extracted from the day's turmoil of work, pleasure and wasted time, turned to the high purpose of attempting to contact the Overself within, made into an oasis of beautiful serenity, provides us with an exalted privilege rather than a difficult duty. Even six months of such practice, rightly, faithfully done and sincerely followed, would enable us to illustrate by personal experience the profound wisdom of Jesus' injunction: "Seek ye first the kingdom of heaven, and all these things shall be added unto you." If we place first things first and keep a correct sense of spiritual values, our worldly existence will itself be placed upon a foundation as firm as a rock.

♣

If the soul obeys no law of gravity to-day, but flies hither and thither, up and down with every pull of circumstance, an hour will certainly arrive in the fullness of time when it shall recover its lost centre. When we can throw aside the passion of random activity for the passion of knowing ourselves, the trick will be done.

♣

The day is barren that brings us no lovely whisper of the Overself nor its quiet fingers caressing our hearts. Yet we grudge the time given to going into silence and permitting the Overself to have its opportunity of service.

♣

A hundred multifarious activities now compete with each other for our time. All seek to rob us of the minutes that might be devoted to the high purpose for which we were born on this planet. "The hours perish and are laid to our charge," is the warning admonition inscribed in Latin on the clock-dial of an old college building at Oxford. Our day has only twenty-four hours upon its dial; we get them free of charge, whether we want them or not; and if we were to yield to all the importunities which are made upon our time we should never make a start with the divine work that faces us, much less arrive at its completion. Each day brings its precious gift of time. Shall we fling away our opportunity through indifference, or shall we account for it honorably? For once we have been taught our true worth and glimpsed our divine possibilities, we will hug time as very life. To waste time is therefore to waste life, but to improve it with musing over matters eternal is to improve life. Those that kill time may live to mourn it. The camera cannot catch any scene for us unless and until we focus it upon the scene. The mind cannot catch hold of the Overself within unless and until we focus it in the direction of that divine being. We spend every hour and every day focusing the mind upon both the important and trivial activities that arise; can we not change around and concentrate for a brief period daily upon the superior reality of the Overself? For if we do, a time will surely come sooner or later when the deeper existence in the depth of the heart will reveal itself to us.

♣

Peace is a costly privilege—to be fought for, attained and won. It comes only from the conquered mind.

♣

We imagine that we are unable to sacrifice a few seconds to the Overself upon the altar of our time, yet we willingly give the months and years to a random activity which leaves us inwardly worse than it found us, and which carries nothing but peace-destroying unquiet to our minds.

♣

Moreover, to be busy is not necessarily to be fruitful of benefit, while to be social is not always an indicator of being sociable. And it has yet to be shown that man was sent into the world to forget himself entirely in a hundred activities. A shrewd and successful man of affairs frequently fails to remember that the world's business would have gone on whether he was born or not; that Nature can always find some man's hands wherewith to work her will; and that until a man knows what he is living for much of his work and most of his pleasures are written on the waves.

♣

Man must turn his eyes inward and begin the most wonderful of all explorations.

♣

We rarely find ourselves in a position where we can indulge in the luxury of leisurely reverie nowadays. For this we are not to blame our stars, our environment and our friends. We accept, without question, the society into which we are born; we submit freely when it impounds and imprisons us. To obtain a recognized place in society we have perforce to pay the price of freedom. Those—whether as commoner or as king—who are prepared, whenever necessary, to disregard the claims of ambition and the criticisms of others at the bidding of the true self, are entitled to ample time for reverie. And the gods so ordain matters that they get it.

♣

Man!—that strange creature who insists on keeping aloof from his Overself.

♣

Applause cannot disturb and disaster cannot interrupt the serene peace which a man who profits spiritually by his leisure may find in his heart. The perilous task of picking out the way back to our native heaven has been made easier for him.

♣

If only people would let go of everything for

a few minutes every day, dropping all tension, relaxing every muscle of the body, reposing the mind and slowing the breath, they might begin to provide the requisite conditions whereby the Overself could make its serenity felt throughout their lives. Thus they would daily learn to withdraw quietly into its peace. Nor would their activities really suffer, even though a little time had been stolen from them. For life would become more balanced, duties would be carried out in a calmer and more collected manner, each crisis or emergency would find them both ready and steady, free from panic.

♣

So the serenity of a dream-haunted leisure may fold around us and keep the coloured patterns of spiritual aspiration from being lost. When the dark worship of Matter in the busy towns wherein we work and live becomes asphyxiating, the memory of that sweet little oasis in inner peace will arise before our eyes and lave us in its waters of healing.

♣

Our use of leisure is significant. Let us turn it, then, to a higher purpose and a diviner value.

CHAPTER XI

HAPPINESS

One mighty desire masters the world. It lives powerfully in the hearts of the rich; it holds the poor. It plays upon the mighty and the humble alike. It grips saints and sinners. It is the desire for happiness.

☘

Happiness! How it draws on the human moths who flit from pre-natal darkness to that other darkness wherein the soul rests!

☘

Our exaltations rise up only at the bidding of rosy circumstances; we have lost the fine art of finding joy in ourselves. Nature bids us pin our hope for happiness to the transcendental life, but necessity seems to drive them towards the transitory existence.

☘

Our thoughts and desires are our betrayers.

They delude us into accepting them as guides to happiness, but in the end they deride us. They drive us hither and thither from birth till death, from every grey dawn till every dark night, and we imagine that we are hurrying to some long sought-for happiness ; one disillusioning day we find that they were really hurrying us away from true happiness. The moral—if there be one—is that only when thoughts cease to hurry us and desires are still shall we be truly blissful.

♣

We repudiate spiritual reality because the earthly dream seems to promise more. Too late ! too late ! do we discover that it is no more than a dream.

♣

I think the shepherd on the hill-side, breathing the fresh air and gazing on the blue sky by day and on the bright stars at night, or listening to the rush of the winds and the tinkle of running brooks, has a princely life in contrast with some overworked and worried wealthy business men I have known, whose minds ran on single tracks, who knew nothing outside their business, who had long lost the ability to get some true and innocent fun out of life, who had become unwilling victims of care's grim oppression, and who were unable to hear the calm, compelling voice of the Overself in the deep silences of their hearts. Envied by their staffs because they belonged to the master class, they had found that their businesses had become their masters. They bought cigarettes to soothe their nerves, but the smoking finished, the effect soon went. Yet they could soothe their nerves by reaching inward to the Overself, and soothe them for ever. They consumed large quantities of alcohol because of its tragic but temporary power to afford release from carking cares, and to dilate the personality. Yet they found but a counterfeit reflection of the serene release which awaited them within their own inner being, the happy enlargement and inward freedom of the Overself which were more solid and more enduring.

♣

While there is inner harmony there is no unhappiness. It is all a question of control of mind, of becoming mentally tuned-in to the Infinite. Happiness must come from within.

♣

The perished civilizations of the past teach an

awful lesson. Chaldea was, and is not. Where now are the hopes and strivings the desires and deeds of every one of those once flesh-and-blood Chaldeans ? The things they strove for are now as assuredly non-existent as themselves. Let us profit by the lesson and possess ourselves of a life that will be true and imperishable, rather than devote all our days to the false and the fleeting.

"I myself am Heaven and Hell," sings the witty Omar. The Sage has the same attitude. He believes that heaven must be found while he is alive. He seeks to achieve happiness by penetrating into his own mind and mastering that.

Blinded by petty distractions, deafened by unworthy outcries, and distracted by pressing necessities, the world's values are largely wrong.

We can snatch pleasure for a few months or a few years, but we cannot hold it enduringly. Happiness is harder to win, for it is inward peace and it must be earned and the calm comes only after the storm. The ephemeral may delude man for a time but it cannot conquer his innate craving for the real happiness. And although he is too busy worshipping gods who are not worth while to take account of the true God, who sits and smiles unnoticed above the hectic hubbub, a day will surely come when he will turn aside with pain and pay his overdue homage, even though it be not until he has paid in the coin of disillusioning experience for the sweets of social existence. Men of wide living, who have tasted most of the pleasures which life can afford only to find them turn bitter on the tongue in the end, may come to perceive this truth; the Sage discovers it by introspection.

♣

Only from complete identity with the living spiritual element within us can come full and lasting happiness. Life itself, with its changing and varying fortunes, provides a bitter initiation into this truth. We need no other teacher to instruct us that within only is abiding good. Yet this truth, so plainly written in our hearts by the hand of our Supreme Father, is generally ignored or condemned.

♣

The guardian angels of many a man tremble

when the fruits of achievement are placed within his grasp, when the plaudits of renown are thrown at him and the honeyed words of praise reach his ear. For success has as many dangers as failure, and souls that could endure the last have been unable to endure the first. Happiness can come only to those who can resist the attentions of both, who can maintain and retain an equanimity of mind which is not to be deceived by the world.

♣

I never envied Gordon Selfridge when I talked to him once in his office high up on Oxford Street, the huge building where he reigned like a king. I felt that I was the proprietor of a better business than he will ever have, one too that will go on paying its high dividends in a distant century when Selfridge and Company, Limited, will be nothing more than a mere name for historians to write three or four lines about.

♣

Ambitions show man a triumphal arch waiting for him at the end of the road, but how often does he not have to drink a cup of bitter gall to the dregs after he has passed this glamorous arch?

How often does not the promised nimbus of leaves to honour him turn out to be a nimbus of pointed thorns upon his head? Thus, even abortive ambition instructs him in a better philosophy than many books. Is it worth while to throw away the true treasures of mind and soul in the race after petty gew-gaws that may prove to be without worth? Is it worth while taking anxious thought how best to compass his little aims, along with the feverish hordes of position hunters, when he has but to commit his entire life into the care of the Overself, which knows better what to do with it than he? Man to-day is cursed by a multitude of mortal concerns that, in the ultimate, need only concern him but slightly, for the Overself knows well how to deal with them. "What shall it profit a man if he gain the whole world, but lose his soul?" asked the wise Galilean.

♣

Notoriety is not fame, and neither makes a man's true happiness.

♣

Trust the Overself—and circumstance will become your providence!

♣

Man imagines his inheritance to consist of the bundle of passions, desires and cares which he carries on his back. Poor creature! He does not know that he can take out letters of probate for a divine estate which is waiting to be his, which will make him truly happy. When a mystic talks of the spiritual exaltation he finds, we wag our heads wisely and suppose that he is being sentimental; it never occurs to us that he may be as matter-of-fact as any realist.

♣

Happiness is the daughter of Truth.

♣

Happiness is native to the Overself. That which we are seeking frantically through a dozen different ways lies unheeded in our lap. Our consciousness is largely limited. Our viewpoint is largely one-sided. For we usually take the viewpoint of the body alone. But if, for a single moment, we could grasp the point of view of the Overself, we might realize that the body is only a little more ephemeral than the dust; why then continue to cling to its toys?

♣

It is strange that though all must travel the

path of life, few care to know whither they are going. We wander from the cradle to the tomb, yet know not our true destination. It is not the tomb ; it is our Overself.

♣

" I cannot sing because I see," wrote that clever man, Israel Zangwill. " I sing because I see," is the answer of the Sage.

♣

Beneath all, like an undertone of true music, are the Everlasting Arms of One Who has been watching and waiting since the beginning of time, Whose patience is without limit and Whose beneficent will must ultimately prevail. Why, then, should we weary ourselves by resisting ; why not rest our own selves in that Universal Self ? If happiness lies anywhere, it must surely lie there ?

♣

The anxious-browed have no other support than prudence ; the spiritually-minded, providence.

♣

The divine song hums all around us, but we are so coarsely constituted that we hear it not.

Only by going into the divine silence may we unstop our ears and catch the elusive melody. Otherwise we must win through to happiness over the bogs of bitter miseries.

"Not this, not this!" cried the Hindu Sage when shown in his trance vision after vision of our worldly life in its most tempting guises. "Not this!" will also become our final verdict upon limited existence once we have penetrated to the diviner life which hides back of it. For then we shall discover that the happiness we sought so fiercely among the sense-binding idols of a day, did exist, albeit not in the places where we thought it to be. Such happiness is life in the Overself, life in the only permanent reality, God, the supreme secret of our constant search. This is the hidden goal of life. It is a star that shines tantalizingly over our heads, while we run after its reflection in muddy pools. The awakening into this absolute understanding is the final beatitude of life. It casts off all that limits us and bestows a blissful liberation upon whilom slaves.

The gospel of optimism is merely the duller

reflection of the bright truth that man's inescapable ultimate fate is spiritual happiness.

♣

The Overself has its own native aim which persists undyingly through all events. So long as we struggle along a direction other than that which it has set us, so long are we unconsciously writing a story of wasted effort. A time will come when, despairing of bringing our all personal desires to perfect fruition, we shall turn about and receive the Overself's purpose into our hearts. And because it shall henceforth bear all our burdens, the peace which shall arise will inform us that we have chosen aright. The purpose of the Overself is to draw us to itself. That is happiness.

CHAPTER XII

SUFFERING

It may be impossible to imagine such an event, but a time will certainly come in the ripening of the soul when we shall recognize that sorrow has not come a day too soon, and that failure is sometimes better than success. Such is the mystery of suffering, life's master paradox.

♣

We look for the cure of our aches and pains, our asthmas and rheumatisms. Yet for the cure of our fevered desires and unworthy ambitions, we do not look.

♣

Why should we, players in the modern spectacle, find that our rewards are so often cups of bitterness and diappointment ? Dark cares and gnawing anxieties lurk behind our brows. We can buy things and we can buy people, but we cannot buy happiness. Golgotha comes to all alike and the hands which dispense suffering spare none. Even Wealth sits at the door of life, hat in hand, begging that this dread thing be removed, while the streets of existence are strewn with the bleached skeletons of the unfortunate, the despairing and the heart-broken. Many, whom life has driven down the dark alleys of unending sorrow, often contemplate the coming of death without undue disturbance. How many have gone out into life, after the youthful years, with great hopes ? And how many have returned with empty hands ? Thus the half-sad, half-glad years of existence pass and are gone.

♣

We make frantic efforts to clutch at the phantom pleasures of this world, but realize through bitter-tasting after-fruits how fleeting they are.

♣

Who that has lived to the full has not known the bitterness of Gethsemane, has not felt the sharp nails of unendurable anguish drive into his own flesh ? The Biblical tragedy is thus enacted anew in a minor degree in almost every life. We try first one alluring thing or place after another or pin our hopes to one attractive person or other; when after much struggle and disillusionment we imagine we have found the elusive figure of happiness, the irresistible hand of ephemerality crashes down on our short-lived joy, while the harsh words hurt our ears: "This too must pass."

♣

The remembrance of our bitter times provides us with private hesitations about the alleged benevolence of God. When suffering squeezes the sweetness out of existence for us, it often squeezes out our faith also. When we are tied to the stake of terrestrial woes, the celestial kingdom of heaven must perforce appear a hollow dream at best and a mocking farce at worst.

♣

He who would heal the wounded souls of others must have first suffered Himself. He only has a right to give words of hope and to pronounce phrases of faith unto men, who has Himself walked wearily through the night of despair and has come at long last out of the shadow of deep melancholy. Because He, too, has lain awake at night sweating in stark agony and fearing the horror of another hopeless day. He may then come to us with balm in His hands and anoint us until the pain departs. Otherwise He comes empty. The bitterness which He once felt may open a door in His heart for other suffering human beings. And then, those who have suffered deeply, whose own hearts have been broken and their hopes withered, may listen sooner to His message than to that of others, no matter how clever, how intellectual, the latter may be.

Whose is this strange and stern Figure which appears at the dark periods of our life and drives us as with whips into the desert of sorrow, there to suffer, to languish and to learn? Who comes and heaps these bitter burdens that we carry, and mercilessly bids us to endure them? Who sits, a silent, sinister figure, at the table of life and plays chess with humanity? Whose is the ghostly form that follows us wherever we go, walking behind us in the streets of the city and across the vestibules of its houses, riding with us into the green countryside or going across the seas? That figure is Fate. We can more easily escape prison for our crimes than escape our fate.

♣

The Overself speaks to man in the only language that his deafened mind cares to understand—

suffering. And it uses as its instrument—fate. It knows that the truths he learns slowly from days of blood and tears are learnt for all time. The lessons may have to be repeated again and again to strengthen their impression, but eventually they are etched so deeply that they can never be forgotten. Then they become more profound and more vital to us than any learnt from the moving lips of Arders ; fate is merely the medium through which the Overself works.

♣

However much the heart may dislike their memory, the mind will one day not regret those long interludes of grief which came as unconscious tutors to teach one to walk wisely among men.

♣

Is fate, then, arbitrary, blind and a force that irresponsibly strikes one man down, whilst it raises another ? If that were so, then the Overself would share the same condemnation, would itself be worthy of conviction as an unjust and irresponsible force. But is it likely that a Power which is higher and nobler than unredeemed man is worse than him in its dealings with us ? The thought is irrational, and those of us who have communed with the Overself know it to be untrue.

♣

"Coincidence" and "accident" are terms which carry a meaning only to the blind materialist, not to the spiritually awakened. For an etheric network covers the universe and ties men to men, men to events, and event to event. The hands that pull and guide this strange net are necessarily invisible, but they are there. The gods have many servants, and all do not wear the flesh.

♣

"The gods ordained it, and it must be so"—Sophocles' *Ajax*.

♣

What, then, is fate? It is our inheritance derived from ancient births of that paradoxical creature, our personality, our ego, our separate self, enfleshed at different times and in different lands farther back than we might care to remember. For we are the legatees of our own long past. The thoughts that gripped our minds in civilizations which are now dead dust, grip us anew in modern

Europe. The acts of good or ill which marked or marred our earlier appearances upon this rotating planet, throw bright sunshine or gloomy shadow over our present years. The long panorama of human life twists its age-old way through the cities and deserts, sending the same persons back again and again to take up the old trail, in the fine and seemingly faint hope of reaching some Canaan of enduring happiness. Life is thus itself a perennial wonder. It disappears from our sight through the grim portals of death, only to reappear again with the fresh spring leaves and the bright-petalled flowers of a new birth. Materialists may talk themselves hoarse in trying to turn this world into a gigantic tomb, but that is because they have not learnt the secret of their own true nature. The body and the body-mind incarnate again and again, but the Overself never. The first are transient, their pleasures and pains will one day disappear with them, but the last is eternal and undying, *for it is Life.*

♣

A superficial mind may find it apparent that the Supreme Creator has played some sort of a joke on man—and a bad joke, too. For man—poor, defenceless creature—is born willy-nilly into this material world, grows up and usually lives at least a third of his numbered days before he begins even to understand that there may possibly be another world of being. And then destiny begins to deal out her cards to him and he may well ask why some are handed to him and not to others. No answer comes, except in the absolute stillness of his innermost being—and he is too busy to listen to that!

The personal ego slips unnoticed out of our world at the body's death and later slips back again into the body of a new-born babe. Bit by bit the old tastes and capacities, the old characteristics, begin to emerge and arrive at fruition with manhood. No memory of the bygone existence remains simply because Nature has wisely and mercifully handed the soul the cup of Lethe to drink, the draught that brings oblivion of the entire past. Yet although the memory of its former acts may pass away, their results on the man and on others remain. Which of us can ever remember a single one of our deeds during the first twelve months of this existence? Yet the later years are merely the onward flow of those months. So, too, although a man may not remember his former lives, his present existence is merely the onward flow of those which have vanished. If Nature were not merciful and gave us no release from those vanished memories, we should be unable to support such a vast shock, extending back to dim antiquity, and we should go completely crazy. But though memory has gone, the influences of the past show their results in our present character, and in the fate portioned out to us.

♣

The keenest minds and the most vigorous intellects have accepted this doctrine. You may ransack the shelves of knowledge in the libraries of the world, but will find no fitter truth than this to explain the varying characters of men. Re-birth rises out of the uncertain atmosphere of theory and establishes itself in the minds of discerning men as a fact. Curled up within the womb of Eastern faiths though it has been, the doctrine of re-embodiment will be cradled in the West as the most philosophical of all explanations of the differences that exist in mankind. We dip into the serial-story of Life with each embodiment, and resume it again in the next instalment. What we are is the outcome of our experiences, but the latter are not to be limited to the brief term of a single existence. Is it better to believe that God has flung us into embodiment to amuse His spare moments by alternately coaxing us with pleasure and then torturing us with pains, or to believe that every birth is but a lesson in the great school of the universe, and that a high wisdom comes slowly to maturity within our minds through this repeated gathering of experiences of every kind with every embodiment ?

♣

The wheel of life revolves and brings us the old experiences in changed form. I know that I am an old scribe ; I do not think I took up the pen with this birth alone. I do not doubt but that I fingered the stylus and the quill in their time. Those earlier lives have given shape and colour to the present one, and brought me back to the old vocation. Our characters and capacities are born with us and earlier years of each life are simply their unfoldment. Wisdom must eventually arise out of our multitudinous experiences and then flow into our attitude towards life.

♣

Fate necessarily arises, too, out of these repeated embodiments, bringing us the results of thoughts and deeds, the fruits of meritorious action and the spiky thorns of wrong-doing. With every year the pen of destiny writes its relentless record on our life. Fate, in fine, is but a veiled law of justice working inexorably in a court invisible to our eyes, and our destiny is written, therefore, less by an unseen hand than by our own. We are not to ascribe it to the arbitrary fiats of some capricious deity; it is self-earned and self-deserved, even though the creative causes stretch far back in time. We get precisely what we deserve; usually we do not think so, but that is because of our blindness, because we are conscious of only a fraction of our past. Nature, however, refuses to excuse us for foolishly imagining that the present is an isolated fragment.

♣

Our ignorance of the fact of re-embodiment, with its consequent corollary of inescapable compensations, does not excuse us in the eyes of the gods of destiny. We are liable to them for our lives down to the last thought. The deeds we drop so irresponsibly do not pass them by so lightly. They know our secret stirrings and we dare hide no purpose from their pitiless gaze. Man is proudly conscious of the fact that he seems to rule this planet; he is not so conscious of the fact that the gods rule man. And so, even when viewing the single existence that he knows, he starts with surprise when the grim forces of hidden justice rise suddenly out of the barren waste and overwhelm him. The power of the gods of destiny encircles and enchains this world, though we know it not. They keep strange records of matters and events which the frail memory of man has entirely forgotten. Moreover, perceiving the personality and nature of man, they can sketch out at birth the exact parabola of his curve of coming experience and foretell the varying co-ordinates of his likely behaviour. Like carven giants, there stand four stupendous beings who guard the confines of the world at the compass-points. Their eyes flash a more awful fire than was ever lighted on any Druid altar, for it is the fire of perfect justice. Few men dare to gaze into that terrible brilliance, which scorches them to the last thought; fewer still fail to move their lips in complaint when their cup of bitter recompense is unexpectedly handed them to be drunk unto the very end. These four hold this world within their majestic power as in a fine web through which not one atom can escape. They employ a host of invisible servants and swift-winged messengers whose strange powers will be understood only by children, so incredible are they to a people that has grown out of the sense of awe which blesses the opening years. These secret legions of the air leap from man to man and tie those unseen threads that run through our complex and mysterious human existence, bringing dire misery to one, or the treasure-chest of fortune to another. They were known to the Greek mind as the Fates and Furies, and to other ancients by less picturesque names, for in the earlier days of our race the screen which hides their domain was but half-drawn.

♣

The times and tides of destiny tarry for no man. The man who blindly imagines that he can spread suffering upon others whilst attempting to work his own selfish will, and get away with it, is to be pitied. Every embodiment will bring him a fresh purgatory, and every death will find him headed for the temporary hell of the wailing ones, until he learns to change in obedience to conscience that slow-waxing voice of many embodiments. If he breaks the rules of life's game, the gods will, in time, break him. "There is no education like adversity," remarked d'Israeli. The leopard cannot change his spots, say the knowing ones, but let him be re-embodied often enough and he shall. So with man. Time can change the face of any temperament and turn evil into good. And what is true for one man, is true for all mankind also. The whole world to-day is passing through a fated epoch of re-adjustments, many painful but still self-earned, and the outstanding figures of its present history are merely the unconscious instruments of Nemesis or the tools of providence.

A mere nobody may yet master the world, if destiny decrees it. We are too prone to judge a man by his past record, whether it be of littleness or greatness, all erring of the indubitable fact that it is not ourselves alone who choose our work and supplies our attainments, but also an over-riding destiny. We take people too much at their surface value and too little at their inner worth. Martin Luther was such a nobody, an unknown and unimportant monk in the little German town of Wittenberg. The world could not see the soul that hid beneath his rough cowl and robe, although it could see the proud pomp of Pope Leo. Luther broke across the attention of Europe and made the papal power reel. Thus he performed an allotted part in the exciting drama which was composed in the history of his day. Napoleon was another such nobody, a hungry junior lieutenant who, before the battle of Toulon, had accomplished nothing. None knew that his mind was habitually occupied with the policies that ought to occupy the mind of a general, but all knew that he was an unimportant, poverty-stricken subaltern who could be disregarded. Then destiny got to work and made him the cynosure of the Western world. Thus, both the monk and the soldier obeyed an overshadowing destiny and carried out its silent dictates. For they had brought over the requisite talents, capacities and character from former existences on earth.

♣

Chance! Two men were travelling on foot in medieval Germany when a tremendous storm suddenly overtook them. Amid the sonorous roll of thunder they both ran for shelter, side by side. Before a safe place could be reached, lightning flashed across their path. One dropped dead almost at the feet of his companion. The latter was totally unharmed. The fates had saved him, his destiny had protected him, for it was bound up with the religious destiny of Europe. That man was Martin Luther. A general walked one sable, moonless night, around a fortification which he was besieging. One of his own sentries challenged him. The general was lost in thought, planning and scheming, as was his wont. His reverie was so profound that he did not hear the challenge. When he was but a few feet away from the sentry the latter fired point-blank at him. The general was thrown to the ground by the force of the shot and lay prone. A minute later he rose quite unharmed. Again the mysterious working of destiny had protected him from explosive death, for he too was linked with the unfulfilled history of Europe. That man was Napoleon Bonaparte. Men may scheme lives as they will, but there remains an imponderable and invincible element that moves of its own accord—the element of fate. Anterior lives throw their dark shadows upon us or light up the years with unforeseen fortune.

♣

The modern world, which prides itself on the all-conquering power of the human will, will eventually have to accept the presence of fate as one of the mighty forces of the universe, just as it has learned to accept the presence of electricity. The wise of every age, both in the East as well as in the West, have subscribed their names in submissive belief to its existence. If, for all that, it remains a profound mystery and the Sages have given out little to the world concerning its working, we need not wander into many words about it, but take thought only for the general principle. Then we shall understand that nothing important happens in our lives by accident, that no event and no person who influences us comes into our existence just casually, and that all is but the out-working of universal justice and intelligence. We shall understand, too, that life is much like that strange Australian weapon, the boomerang. We throw out harmful deeds and evil thoughts against other men, but time passes, and lo—what we have sent out returns again, hurting our own bodies and poisoning our own minds, all being brought back by the irresistible forces of Nature. We should, then, cease to beat our heads in complaint against the walls of circumstance, or to murmur loudly against whatever powers there be. We shall give entrance to the thought that we ourselves have created most of our destiny.

♣

We cannot mention the word fate without dragging in the ancient controversy that links it with the opposing term free-will, and that again with the arts of prediction. So paradoxical is the entire subject that we find master men of action like Cæsar and Napoleon, whom the world regards as apostles of free-will and self-reliance, to be convinced believers in the dominant power of destiny. We may spend many fascinating but perplexing hours pondering upon these age-old questions. If destiny exists, are we to relax into helpless lethargy because free-will is but a dream? Like all questions of this kind, the answers of both proponents and opponents contain but half-truths. A complete solution of this problem will not oppose the replies, but rather accept them and endeavour to make them fit into one another. A balanced judgment can reconcile a belief in fate with the perception of the necessity of individual effort. To hold to either position as being completely satisfactory is to indicate that there is a kink in one's nature, as well as to betray but a superficial understanding of existence. If man is held in the grip of pre-ordained events, it is equally true that there is an element of freedom somewhere or he would never be able to achieve the high purpose set him by spiritual evolution.

♣

The East has exaggerated the power of fate. The West has exaggerated the power of free-will. A saner view will combine a vigorous unholding of man's innate strength with due credit to the pre-ordained fiats of destiny. Thus we may accept the two-edged doctrine of self-created *kismet* and drink the unpalatable draught if needs be, but we may also affirm that the soul which is struggling to alter itself, is likewise struggling to alter its fate. Thus the knots of our lives are primally tied by our qualities of character and capacity, and by no other hands. We bear within us the dispenser of our destinies, the arbiter of our good and ill. Let it be true that a secret fate overrules our little throws and lesser efforts, and that the winning of the game not infrequently depends upon its smile or frown. But we must also recognize that this fate is only ourselves in another guise. It is the fruit—good or bad—that has fallen off the tree planted in former embodiments. We must needs accept and eat this fruit and if it is too tart for our taste, then we shall learn to plant better seeds and work the orchard of life in a worthier manner. After all, if it be man who creates his own fate, the logical conclusion is that he himself can influence it. Here logic coincides with truth. To make destiny all-powerful, capable of being influenced neither by man or angel, is to render this great truth harmful and not helpful to man.

♣

The Orientals, holding as a central tenet of

their religions that fate is remorseless, because it furnishes the virtuous with an exact reward and pursues the wicked until they are punished, have sunk into a supine fatalism which renders them credulous and pitiable victims of every fortune-teller. The arts of prediction flourish apace in the East, and now rapidly spread their tentacles throughout the Western lands too. Professional predicters are to-day members of a thriving trade. The lack of anything stable in the framework of the modern world, the insecurities and despairs, the tragedies of fortunes lost and employment gone, the romantic sex notions bred by modern cinemas and stories, all these send the human race to the so-called seers—less perhaps because it has full faith in them than because it knows not where else to turn. That hope which is supposed to spring eternal in the human breast induces it to draw a slender comfort from the possibility of hearing that Fortune's revolving wheel may perchance soon turn in their favour. The pit of uncertainty yawns beneath their feet. Others attempt to increase their existing fortunes by using costly prognostications, hardly awake to the fact that anyone able to predict future results accurately enough to make fortunes for others, would best prove it by making his own fortune first. The absurd claims to complete prescience made by many professionals, can only help to strengthen the case of their critics. Although it is true that an unbiased and scientific study of the major predictive arts may enable one to discover a deeper meaning behind the words coincidence and accident, it is not true that they will enable one to become possessed of the omniscience of a god.

♣

If disaster threatens you, do not pray to be saved ; pray rather for more strength, more faith, more courage. Save yourself, and let the gods of destiny do what they will with your body. Thus you attract the help of unseen forces.

♣

A wise man knows when to bow his head before inexorable, invincible destiny and when to grapple with it persistently. He will know when to bear patiently with apparently maleficent destiny that cannot be altered, do what he may, but he will also know that it matters less what his horoscope holds than what his soul holds. If it is wisdom to believe in destiny and re-embodiment, it will be higher wisdom to believe in the power of man's inmost self, the Overself, to trust to that power, to relax and let it deal with problems, trials, difficulties and despairs. It is better even to forget the ideas of many enfleshments and overshadowing fate, if they are going to enslave us into helpless lethargy, as they have enslaved so many Orientals. We need to forget every limitation that such notions bring in order to obtain firm faith in the possibility that the kingdom of heaven exists for us here and now. We must let go, in mind, of dismal fate, or of all coming troubles in which irresponsible fortune-tellers have made us believe, and find the inner freedom of the Overself. Even were we immutably preordained to undergo predicted disasters, our reaction to them is not preordained. Events may be fixed by unseen powers, but our attitude towards them is not.

♣

Worry is spiritual short sight. Its cure is intelligent faith.

♣

Life, looked upon as an education in wisdom, seems to have some sense in it after all.

♣

Man himself is free, eternally free; only his

body and mind are subject to destiny. The wisest course is to seek out and claim this freedom, then all destiny is forced to let go its grip.

♣

The weak man worries over his horoscope, but the wise man tears it up. He knows that the Sun, Moon, Mars, Saturn and Jupiter are all within him. "The fault, dear Brutus, is not in our stars, but in ourselves, that we are underlings," said Shakespeare. Every planet becomes an auspicious star that helps and never hinders once he has struck the road of a divinely harmonious life. Nature is the friend of man, not his enemy, and readily proves it when he ceases to war with her, but places his life in the hands of her master, the Creator. What have we done to Nature that she should wish us evil? Take fortune quietly and misfortune still more quietly. The effect of troubles will then depend precisely on the way you think about them. To regard events and men in this way is to realize that opposition is also opportunity. It is an opportunity to gain greater faith, greater courage, and greater wisdom. Such gain will replace whatever loss of things may have occurred to you, and thus provide compensation. Change your view-point from the common angle, and reflect those divine qualities which lie hidden within you—be positive, be affirmative, and above all be calm. Then, whilst you pick your way through the briars and thorns that an apparently malign fate has planted in your path, you need not let those briars and thorns get inside you. Not a single protective quality of the divinity in whose image you are made can ever be lost, or hurt, or cast aside. They are all there within you, and when you cannot control things outside, call these optimistic qualities into expression and then you will certainly control their effects upon you. Why entertain negative thoughts when you may have bright ones?

♣

Striving helps to draw one onwards, tests make and evolve a man. Therefore it is often better not to know one's future, but to depend on inner resources wherewith to meet every event. The mind must keep its native balance, and if the unready majority saw all, their minds would become unbalanced. The Creator's workings are shrouded in mystery for a good purpose, and it is better to live in awe until the hour of illumination arrives, until one has come into alignment with the Overself. It is better to rein in the inquisitiveness that would peer into time, and become inquisitive about that which transcends time. Seek out the Overself, come to the cognisance of your true inner being, and you shall find the serene contact of the eternal. Then you shall never mutter against your dark fate, the cataract film will drop from your eyes, and in that sacred hour you shall live enthroned, protected, secure with the wings of divinity enfolded around you. Why then trouble the soothsayers and let them drag you down to anxious curiosity, to a running hither and thither for scraps of well-being, when the ineffable condition of supreme and constant serenity awaits you ? Why seek the less when the greater lies within reach of your hand ? To pry anxiously into the coming years is to confess your lack of faith, your inability to trust the higher power. Trust it, and in the measure of your faith it shall act accordingly unto you. Within the sanctuary of your ever-present Overself, all woes will disappear, all enigmas receive their silent answer, all problems disappear, all concern for past or future be cancelled out, and all uncertainties and fears take their unregretted dismissal. This is what Jesus meant when He bade His disciples take no thought for the morrow ; they did not need to, for they had entrusted their lives to His higher power, a power which could very well take care of the coming years for them. And because the Heart of Being is Benevolence, know that your life is no less dear to the Supreme Father than it is to you. Listen deeply to the inner Monitor ; let the voiceless speak, for there is " One who is carrying both this world and your burdens, not you."

♣

Once when Jesus walked with soft tread on the Galilean shore, he turned to those that were with Him and said : " If ye will trust the Father as I have trusted him, then shall ye find the kingdom of heaven. If ye will live from day to day as though he were with you and dwelt in you, then will ye be truly about your Father's business. Woe ! woe ! is with them that do not trust him."

♣

In this high mood, then, we may know how to suffer and how to enjoy, and we may turn our faces towards the morrow as its illumined master and not as its troubled victim. Thus may we live in the divine present.

CHAPTER XIII

SELF AND OVERSELF

I would give a new Beatitude to the world! "Blessed is the man who has found his own self!"

Gaze into your own heart, O Man, and see what a pitiful concourse is there gathered! The fickle figure of Joy walks arm-in-arm with wan-eyed Depression, and both seem inseparable friends. The restless panther of Lust moves up and down that narrow space, while in the far corner that white-robed, outgrown child Innocence weeps over past memories. Care, a grey and bent greybeard, staggers along under his enormous burden, his tired bleary eyes casting envious glances now and then at Peace, who sits in quiet content as in a rose-bower. Ha! in bustles strong, self-important Ambition, whose cloaked form hides many a heartache of disappointment .... And so one could go on, peering here and there into your heart, revealing all those alien intruders who have taken possession of your abode, for know, they are not yourself, nor is their home your real Heart.

"Man, Know Thyself!" All the wisdom of bygone ages, all the wisdom that unborn ages shall ever discover, is summed up in this one phrase. Three words—yet they cover all life! I defy you to find three others that shall better this divine counsel to man. They were inscribed in marble over the most sacred Mystery-temple of ancient Greece, they were written down on palm-leaves by the Sage-Rishees of Indian antiquity, and they were silently echoed during high initiations within the Great Pyramid itself.

There is in the soul of every man something infinitely greater and grander than he knows, more than he ever dreamed of. We hold hard to the outer husk of body consciousness because we are ignorant of the divine kernel it contains. We have wandered the broad waters and crusted lands of this globe; it is now time to turn in our tracks and explore ourselves—the most wonderful of all globes. Here lie vast continents of the mind and here stretch illimitable seas of the heart, hardly travelled and barely recorded in the books. The most astounding discoveries will come when our scientists turn away for a while from metal and stone and electricity to examine and explore the nature of self within the laboratory of Man. " I and all mankind, beneath our garb of commonplaceness, conceal enigmas," wrote Herman Melville, intuitively.

Self-ignorance sits on the thrones of the world of knowledge. Our guides run feverishly hither and thither to pick up scraps of information about this and that, yet give but little time to consider the far more important question: "*Who is this being that seeks this information?*"

No lesser study than self is worthy of the highest powers of man's mind. For he could not perceive the world outside him and he could not register his impressions of it through his five senses, did his self not exist to receive this perception and those impressions. In short, the world would not exist for him did he not himself exist first. Scientists already know, through the experiments of hypnotism, that the real seeing agent in sight is not the physical organ of the eye, but rather the mind that uses that organ. In short, it is the mind that works the eyes. They have yet to discover what it is that works the mind. And when they do that they will come into contact with the real self of man, the being out of whom both mind and body derive their existence and maintain their lives.

Immanuel Kant has given the philosophic world ample proof that the universe is really a mould into which man has thrown his consciousness, and that its ultimate existence is inside our minds. He demonstrated this by the strictest deductions and the most careful considerations. So deep and so close was his reasoning that few can ever venture to follow him, while fewer still have ever understood him. Beyond and above he placed the real world, the Infinite, the Absolute, which he declared unknowable by human intellect. In that he was obviously correct. But beyond the logic-machine of brain, the Sages point to a higher faculty, which illumines the thick darkness that envelops it, and they declare that those in whom this faculty is awake find as a reality what for Kant was but a proved theory. The practical import of all this metaphysics is that it opens up the possibility of freeing man from the continual domination of his material surroundings. He may set the external world at defiance, if only he can penetrate to this interior world of being, because he may live an independent existence within the latter. So far he knows but a fragmentary part of his inner being, where vast strata of power and intelligence lie latent.

♣

But this being is apparently the most elusive thing in the world. "How would you be buried?" asked Criton of Socrates, shortly before the latter's death. "Just as you please," replied the sage, "if you can but catch me and I not elude your pursuit!" Science, which has put in so much research along a multitude of lines, has yet to find out who and what we are. For it is something that no instruments, however costly, will ever get hold of and that no telescope will ever sight. Yet the scientist can obtain the means necessary to perceive this being gratis, for they are all contained within himself, in his own mind and heart. That real self is hidden in the recesses of man's soul, where no eye of flesh ever penetrates. If the curtains are to be thrown aside, as they can be, then the means used must be subtle enough to reach these depths.

♣

The means used are then nothing more than thought and feeling. We scatter our thoughts in a wholly reckless manner, and we let our emotions change with every few minutes; the power that might be retained by their concentration is usually lost. Our minds are therefore in a continuous state of vibration, and but rarely at rest. These are the real causes why we are so tied to the material world that we are blinded by it, and miss the spiritual reality that awaits our attention within the regions of the soul.

♣

This is not the place to describe a psychological method in detail, but the principles that underlie it can be described. When the mind is deeply engaged in a train of thought, it tends to become unconscious of external surroundings as concentration deepens. When this condition is carried to a profound extent, then the mind becomes one-pointed. If, at this degree, the subject of the meditation could be somehow dropped, the ensuing vacuum would swiftly cause the hidden world of man's soul to arise and fill it. In that apparent emptiness he would become aware of a new visitant, his Overself. Such is the essential principle behind this process of self-knowing.

♣

The difficulty of concentrating the thoughts sufficiently is followed by the greater difficulty of suspending the thoughts altogether. The first is to be overcome by steady daily practice, a little at a time, until the dogged persistence is able to drive one's wandering thoughts to a fixed inner centre for a time. The second can be accomplished by a clever psychological device originally revealed by the Sages of hoary antiquity, but afterwards lost to the world for many centuries; it has now been recovered and made known by the Maharishee of South India. It consists in taking as the subject of meditation the inquiry, "*Who Am I?*" The mind must centre itself upon this single question, pressing deeply inward in the effort to discover the elusive inhabitant of the body. If the concentration is complete and the persistence undiminished; if the inquiry is conducted in the correct manner; if the person is really sincere; then an extraordinary thing will happen. The mental current of self-questioning, the attempt to ferret out what one really is, the watching of one's thoughts in the earlier part of the process, ultimately pins all thinking down to the single thought of personal existence. "I" is the first thought sprayed up by the spring of life's being, but it is also the last. As this final thought is held in the focus of attention and questioned in a particular way, it suddenly disappears and the Overself takes its place, overwhelming both questioner and question in its divine stillness. Throughout the whole course of meditations the Overself within had waited and watched, biding its time, for it is timeless. The principle behind this process of tracking self to its lair can be explained by a simple analogy: a dog can trace out and find its own master amidst a crowd of people by the sense of scent alone; similarly the intellect can trace out and find its true master—the Overself—by following the trail of the sense of "I" to its source.

♣

This technique is perfectly sound psychologically and spiritually, although it involves certain facts scarcely credible yet to modern science, but destined to be amply proved well within this century. It traces the intellect back to its true origin, and reveals the true nature of the personal ego. It restores the long-lost balance of man's trinity—body, mind and soul—which is now in an upside-down condition. It replaces Consciousness upon its rightful throne deep within the Heart, and dethrones that usurper, the brain. It solves stubborn questions which have puzzled the thinkers among men since reason first evolved. It dissolves all necessity of argument, for it offers a first-hand experience that settles the question of the soul once and forever. It makes it possible for us to understand to-day, in this practical bustling twentieth century, what has been echoed back to us from the words of outstanding spiritual Teachers of former ages. And by enabling one to enter into the basic centre of man, that place of absolute rest, effulgent wisdom and silent harmony, it reveals the identity between the blessed Nirvana of Buddha, the Kingdom of Heaven of Jesus, the Liberation of Sri Krishna and the Realm of Osiris. It plumbs the mind's depths and brings about one's inner return to the hidden element out of which both it and the body were really created. That element is none other than the Absolute Being, the Underlying Spirit which subsists eternally amid the births and deaths of mortal men and material worlds.

♣

A daily effort to meditate along these lines is

worth while, because it produces eventually the fine sublimate of the Overself. To set aside a little time to do something quite opposite to the ordinary routine of living, brings a new influence into the working hours, so potent is this practice. The Overself waits with open arms, but few care to take their time, whether it be leisure or the whole of life, and pitch it into the flames of sacrifice. Give the Overself some of your time and much of your devotion, and it will eventually give itself to you.

♣

No education will ever be a complete one or a true one that omits this essential preparation for the business of living. None are too young nor too old to practise it. No disappearance of the hatred and selfishness, the cruelty and greediness, the bitterness and bestiality, which afflict the human race and turn this once-fair planet into a horror among the stars, can ever be looked for whilst man persists in identifying himself wholly with his material body. No eternal reform will ever renovate mankind whilst we remain, Prometheus-like, chained to the rock of matter. Mankind, during its long wandering down the ages, has wandered too far outwards from its spiritual centre ; whether we like it or not, there is now no way of re-establishing our lost balance and harmony other than by turning inwards again towards that centre. Various ways have been shown by past Teachers, but the technique here propounded is the one that seems to have the most universal application in this day and age ; for we live in an intellectual epoch and this way uses as its instrument of attainment the very intellect itself—heretofore regarded by most mystics as the enemy of spiritual achievement !

Man has largely withdrawn his faith from God, but he cannot withdraw his faith from self ! If he has deserted what seems to him problematic and doubtful, he can never desert the fact of his own conscious existence. Nothing is more certain to him than the certainty of " I am ! " The path of inquiry into the nature of self is therefore one which deals with ascertainable matters and not with a supposititious Deity. It should make appeal to this rational age on this ground, if on no other. If a doctrine is to be at all convincing to the modern brain, it must have its roots both in reason and experience. Though the educated world has said farewell to blind faith, it has not to investigation. And it may explore the labyrinths of recorded thought in its quest of Truth, yet not find a suggestion more potent than this. The foolish materialist and the fanatical religionist may reject it, but that will be because they both prefer foolishness and fanaticism to truth.

♣

It is we who have erected the screens that shut us out from the Overself; and therefore it is we who must pull down those screens. Somewhere in the depths of our being dwells this august and eternal existence; it is here within; it is the supreme purpose of all living; and so long as we insist on ignoring it our condition will remain truly pathetic, for we shall remain involuntary exiles from our true Home-state. We do not realize what buried treasure lies within us. Those who have come to know themselves are richly rewarded. They feel their inward kingship and know that weakness and want can no longer be theirs; that sin and stupidity are cob-webs that were long permitted to cling on, but have now been cast off; and that the secret treasure they have found will abide with them to eternity, uneaten by moths and unstolen by thieves.

♣

Let us try to know him upon whom we base our

whole existence ; let us seek out this personal ego, this " I am " to whom we tie all our threads of hope and fear, of purpose and desire.

We suffer because we are astray from our centre. When we shall remember who we are and return, sorrow will drop off with no thoughts to feed it, as the leaves drop off in autumn with no sap to feed them.

Life refuses to yield its sublimest secret to the lazy. If you want to find out its true meaning, why, then you must begin to look for it. And the place to look is within.

We know ourselves as human beings, but we have yet to know ourselves as spiritual beings.

When all the scholars and savants and theologians have written the last word of their varied theories and commentaries ; when the great philosophers have had their lengthy say; we shall still remain baffled before the mystery of the Overself. It is inexplicable. It is the self-created ray of light out of the Absolute Darkness. It is the nearest that any human being can get to God. All that can be truly said of it may be contained in three words—*The Overself IS*. We must bow our humbled heads before it, for we cannot explain it. Religion rests on the proposition that the Supreme Creator is to receive our best thoughts and the profoundest movements of our hearts. But the Creator is just beyond the ken of the average man, a Mystery of Mysteries, and no road stretches open towards Him save that of intense faith. The man who is born religious can give this faith, but the man who loses his religion with his youth is often unable to do so. In fact the traditional views of religion have lost much of their cogency for the modern man. How to create faith in and love towards a Being who is unknown and unknowable, it does not answer. But the path of spiritual self-inquiry rests on a simple fact—our own conscious existence as individual selves. It is a path with a goal plus a sure reward. It gradually leads a man from the lesser transient self to that glorious centre where abides his Overself, which is none other than the ray of God in him. Thus he may approach God, but he needs no blind credulity for the task; rather does it demand some intelligence.

Attempt to explore within for your Overself, and one day you may experience it.

Let us attempt to find Truth at first-hand within ourselves and not depend so much upon the second-hand ministrations of other men, nor the third-hand veilings of book and Bible. We should stand up on our own feet, and not walk through life on the thoughts of others. We should take our stand upon our own inherent divinity, for a second-hand illumination has already lost some of its value when it reaches our ears. The final reference is, and always must be, within. Truth never publishes its final statement, reserving that for those who will adventure into its home.

Before you are able to help others, you must first be able to help yourself. You will be able to take the souls of other men in fee and pawn, but only after you have gathered in sufficient resources of your own. You must be your own friend first before you can befriend others. Whilst you stand as a spiritual beggar before the door of life, it is foolish to talk of giving alms to others. Be that rarity, the man who has sought and found the Overself; then you shall have gifts in your store which a million other men cannot give; then you shall know how to serve mankind unostentatiously, secretly, without acts and without words, yet so effectively that you remould men and hence their lives.

♣

The Overself is seated in the soul of man like an Oriental goddess seated on her throne of lacquered wood—calm, imperturbable and untouched by the hurried ways of our excited existence. Each man is thus, in very truth, his own god, his own teacher, his own prophet. Is it not comforting at least to know that amid all the troubling passions, brooding depressions and ungovernable thoughts of our nature, there yet exists a central core of quiet? Is it not worth while to make the effort that will one day bring us to rest within the cradle of being like a new-born babe, serenely trusting that which above all else is worthy of trust? Is it not better to become for ourselves an oracle of divinity, a channel of sublime inspiration, and an ambassador of the ever-beckoning Absolute?

♣

He who can conquer thoughts has conquered the world. This is the only victory worth having, for it delivers all other spoils into his hands. The mastery of thought is the quintessence of the mastery of the world. There in the realm of hidden things, in the region of unseen forces, are the real sources of power. Whoever contacts these regions in the right way can make and unmake both men and movements. He can live unknown and work in secrecy, but his efforts will strike home. His results will be sure. He will attain a sublime confidence yet withal feel an overwhelming humility, for he will understand what exalted Beings are working through him. The irresistible forces work silently. When Jesus told His hearers that if they sought the kingdom of heaven first, all other things would be added unto them, it was not only a general statement—as so many of His phrases were—but also a definite one.

♣

We are all responding to the gravitational pull of the Overself, and if the way is long the end is sure. For man, the real man, the Overself, is truly made in the image of God, as the Biblical phrase puts it, and the divine qualities which he possesses can never be destroyed. First we begin to feel the Overself's guidance in the gentlest of ways, then we hear its mystic murmurs mingled with our crowd of thoughts, finally we are impelled to follow its strange promptings. We may resist it to-day, but a morrow shall surely dawn when, on bended knee, we shall be forced to surrender. Nature herself is in no hurry. She has plenty of time wherein to accomplish her purposes with man. If the day is delayed, nevertheless it is certain. Man cannot play false to his heredity for ever. Spawned of the gods, he must return to them.

♣

This starry self is the final essence, the life-giving principle within us. Its departure from the body means death. But because it is the very Heart of man and inseparable from him, he need have no fear. It is all-wise, all compassionate and all beautiful, and because it is the ineffable ray of God within us it is also immortal. So long as God lives, we, too, shall live on.

THE EPILOGUE

Were the world's leaders and the masses who follow them ready to accept the better way, to have the faith and daring to try the Golden Rule, their problems would melt down, all Nature would co-operate and the hidden powers would come to their aid. Were they ready to accept spiritual values as a worth while standard, they might see their dreams of happy, prosperous and peaceful lands come true. Were they courageous enough to challenge the gods in this striking manner, they would not, they could not, be disappointed.

But the dead hand of the past drags them back. Yesterday has gone but not for them. Why not let the dead bury their dead, and follow a new sun and begin anew? The ancient Mayas of Central America carried this to the point of burning all their personal effects at intervals. There is some sense even in this apparently senseless custom. We can always make fresh starts, always turn with hope to the Infinite that brought us into being, and really reared us.

The world is in the throes of a new birth. We

experience the agony of it all right, but the joy of deliverance must follow. Meanwhile it is well that we realize that this planet whereon we are camped for a time, is not our true home. We are errant wanderers and there is no rest for us until we return repentantly to the Overself.

The last word was written. The task with which I had been entrusted on Arunachala was finished. I had faced the world long enough during my survey; it was now time to turn my head and face the peak itself.

I sat on the rough stone step outside my hut, stirred my cup of Darjeeling tea and, comforted by its attractive aroma, contemplated my surroundings. The old Lemurian "fire-hill" as the people called it, rose up from the very fringe of the little clearing in the growth of cactus and clumps of brush.

A beady-eyed green lizard gazed down at me from the hut wall to which it clung pertinaciously, even as I had gazed up at the peak's flattened head. A black crow descended upon the roof, croaking vigorously and vociferously, in search of the crumbs which it knew had been scattered at that hour. A female monkey with twitching yellow eyes passed by as she jumped from boulder to boulder, her happy youngster clinging to her breast with both dun-coloured arms. She reached the artificial pond and deposited the infant on the bank, threw herself down and eagerly lapped up the water. Following this she entered and cooled her heated body in the water, splashing noisily.

As a final accompaniment of sound, the persistent hum of mosquitoes made itself heard, mingling with the perpetual chorus that came from the trees where a hundred chirping sparrows had gathered.

My eyes roamed over the irregular landscape until they reached the horizon of the brown hills. I was waiting patiently for that diurnal descent of the sun which fills the world with coloured beauty and my heart with soft tranquillity.

When at length Ravi began to descend from his flaming throne in the bright Indian sky and shed a rosy light on the gaunt solemn hill, the latter took on a livelier aspect. Its desolate appearance went and the rocky, debris-covered face of the slope actually glowed with cheerful ruddiness.

The sky was irregularly touched to a tender rose, whose reflection flickered down upon the light-flooded land. Time travelled on. Pearly opalescent shadows showed themselves in large patches against the rose in the heavens. I watched the warm-coloured rays fade away from the topmost point of the peak. The ungainly outline of sprawling Arunchala turned sombre against the evening sky. The sinking sun had ceased its effort to burnish the landscape with gold.

I thought back to that far time in our planet's history when gigantic earthquakes piled the rocky mount high above the ground and made it a part of Lemuria, the companion continent of Atlantis. Lemuria to-day moulders under the dark waters of the Indian and Pacific oceans, turning those ancient seas into gigantic mausoleums for dead cities and vanished races. Its surviving detached fragments and cyclopean relics are scattered over the southern world.

And I thought how Nature is not sentimental over transient human life. When whole groups of peoples defile her body and descend into monstrous wickedness, she has not hesitated to destroy them with awful cataclysms. It is no superstition. If we can accord a mind and intelligence to the self in our own bodies, why should we not accord a mind and intelligence to the self in the Earth, whence our bodies derive and whither they must return ? It is not less rational to think that a Directing Mind, a Planetary Soul, inhabits our Earth, than it is to think that a directing mind inhabits our own bodies, for flesh and dust are merely two different forms of Matter.

The day had fallen. The jagged rocks and piles of boulders of Lemuria's mute relic were now hardly visible. Arunachala was about to disappear. Its silhouette gradually faded as the Indian twilight swiftly increased. Finally, the Light of Asia was extinguished. Darkness, complete and unrevealing, beset me.

Still I sat on the step, loath to turn back across the threshold and light my waiting lamp. The twilight hour had worked its ancient witchery on me. I could not stir. The beauty of eventide had gently stolen into my senses and through them into my mind. I felt that if Nature could be pitilessly cruel, as she might have seemed to those distressed Lemurians, she could also be unbelievably kind.

I knew only that the sublime beauty and serene atmosphere had percolated into my inmost heart. The body passed into a steady posture as though it were entranced. I sat there like an enchanted man, the eyes open and unblinking like the eyes of a nocturnal bird, seeing and yet not seeing the first fireflies that darted through the air. The hidden bud of the soul broke open and revealed the wonderful flower within. I became aware of an inner blissful world. I forgot the outer world in order to remember my inner self. It was a silent reverie so intense that the peace we sometimes experience during that untroubled minute of delectable borderland between waking and sleeping, was but a hint of it.

Every physical faculty was lulled in delicious repose, every wandering thought was quieted, as I lifted myself out of the foaming river of superficial existence to sit upon its felicitous bank.

The hours passed unchimed and unrecorded. Face to face with the Divine Silence, I learnt the final message of Arunachala. It was the hopeful message of man's eternal, indestructible goodness. For at the very centre of his being dwells God.

PEACE TO ALL BEINGS